The authors

Tizian Baldinger, born 1982, is a Swiss artist, thinker and entrepreneur.

Timon R. Böse, born 1980 in Berlin, is a historian, art historian and author.

N.N. is an anonymous superstar of the international art scene.

Everything for Art

How to be a successful artist

Tizian Baldinger and Timon R. Böse

with

N.N.

Impressum

First published in Germany in 2020
Original title "Alles für die Kunst"

Translated by Ruth Butterfield

www.everythingforart.co
www.boese-verlag.de

Timon R. Böse Onlineverlag
Auf dem Grat 31
14195 Berlin
Germany

Copyright © by Tizian Baldinger & Timon R. Böse

First Edition, Berlin 2021
ISBN: 978-3-949037-03-0

Printed by CPI books GmbH, Leck, Germany.

"Art is a religion."

"Some believe in it and others don't."

Table of contents

About this book

Artists such as Jeff Koons, Damien Hirst, and Banksy have completely seen through the art system and play with it like a virtuoso plays a piano. Although their work regularly stimulates the current art discourse, they do not share the secrets of their success with young – and sometimes perplexed or frustrated – artists. Isn't it astonishing that there is still no standard work for artists? Instead, there are a few how-to books that do a poor job of motivating artists to keep going. It's as if they're cheering on a group of soccer players who don't even know the rules of the game. The main thing is that the fans are yelling.

And this is where the book "Everything for Art" comes into play: The two authors got together with a world-famous artist and asked for some advice. From these conversations – supplemented with input from fellow artists, gallery owners, collectors, and curators, as well as their own rich experiences in the art world – this book was written.

It's not a conventional how-to manual, because it doesn't try to motivate as many people as possible and make them happy. But neither is it a classic textbook that regurgitates existing knowledge. Rather, it is a pioneering work, written from the active artist's perspective of an insider. It is written with the aim of providing the reader with an overview of the current art system that is as comprehensible, structured, and objective as possible. It tries to be helpful and practical without ignoring the fact that success eludes many artists not because of a lack of talent but because of a lack of compatibility with the current art system.

Preface

"I don't have time to read this book or contribute anything for the preface. I'm sure you two will manage without me.

Good luck,
N.N."

These sobering remarks come from an e-mail from our mentor. They are his or her very own words, as are all the italicized quotes in this book. Our mentor wants to remain anonymous. He or she is a great artist, world famous, and known by everyone, and so had no need to be our advisor for this book "Everything for Art." But how did it come about in the first place? We did, in fact, make a list of successful artists we respected and who we considered potential advisors for our book. And, with our first request, we reached for the stars and fate rewarded us. We still don't know why this artist accepted. We only met three times. We then had to compile and distill the contents of this book from our intense conversations and discussions, one of them over copious amounts of alcohol, but also from the few terse exchanges of correspondence and a few past interviews. The original language of this book is German, because it is our native language, but that does not mean that the artist also speaks German.

Our star artist gave us his or her blessing as well as words. Both are more than this person is willing to give most other people. But hold on, we did actually forget two things: First, we were assured sole rights to the book and second, the artist's lawyer presented us with a non-disclosure agreement that would charge us a six-figure sum if we divulged the artist's name. That was the deal.

The idea for this book originally came from Tizian Baldinger, who has been an artist for over a decade and who is from Switzerland. Tizian loves art, but unlike many other artists, he is not addicted to it. That's why he was able to describe the art system so soberly here. Being an aspiring young artist, he is much closer to some of the problems of the art world that the successful artist has long forgotten or that may have been quite different in his or her youth in the last century. During his studies at the HFBK (Hamburg University of Fine Arts), he noticed that there was no textbook of any use to young artists who wanted to take a professional approach to their career. So he decided to write one. The only problem was: He's an artist, not an author. Tizian was able to gather a lot of experience, but this wasn't the same as writing a book.

This is where Timon R. Böse came into the picture, a Berlin author who had himself gained years of experience in the art industry as a curator and art historian. He is also highly familiar with the world of artists. He has worked with many international creative minds in the past. What's more, he and Tizian have known each other for what feels like an eternity.

And so, together with the successful artist, we two friends formed perhaps one of the strangest teams in the history of specialist literature. Three weirdos from the art world who collected their experiences in a book – and one of them only talked, without writing or even reading what had been written. This book was therefore written down exclusively by Tizian Baldinger and Timon R. Böse.

A word of warning: This book is hard work. It won't necessarily make you happy, because it doesn't sugarcoat anything. The book is also not meant to motivate you, but to accompany you on your own path and make you aware that you may have an idealized or poorly differentiated view of the art world. The art world is a complex system, but not a closed book, as some assume or claim. It is therefore less the case that secrets need to be disclosed and more the case that seemingly arbitrary processes and correlations in the art system need to be revealed. And finally: There are many different ways to become a successful artist and at least as many different definitions of successful.

Remember: Successful is not the same as happy.

This book focuses on the future internationally successful artist. The journey is tough, and it requires some sacrifices. Ultimately, you have to decide for yourself whether it is worth it – or not.

We would like to thank our anonymous mentor, and also our many friends and supporters from the art world – and from the other worlds, too. Everything for art!

Tizian Baldinger & Timon R. Böse, October 2020

1. The basis

First, a few basic things need to be defined, so that we can then achieve a deeper understanding of the contemporary art world. The terms briefly defined in this chapter and at the beginning of the next are essential to understanding the later chapters of the book.

When art is referred to in this book, it means fine art, such as painting, sculpture, performance, and so on. Folk art, music, dance, theater, opera, and so on are not covered here.

1.1. Art

Every era has its art. However, the evaluation of art can also change retroactively. In rare cases, art may not have been recognized as such in its time, or may have remained undervalued and only become part of the artistic canon or more highly valued at a later point. The following applies: artistic canon = recognized art. The artistic canon can fluctuate.

If you want to be part of the current artistic canon, then you need to align yourself with it. That is, you first need to understand the canon. Consequently, you need to develop a deep understanding of art. You think you know what art is? This is not about your opinion, your view of art, but the view of the artistic canon. You need to understand the artistic canon. That doesn't mean you have to like it. But you have to understand it.

The easiest way to do this is to study art. Studying art is almost unavoidable today anyway, but more on that later.

You need to get an overview of contemporary art. You have to go to countless exhibitions to find out what exists in your present and what existed in the past.

And it is very important to note: If it says art on the outside, it doesn't necessarily mean there is art on the inside. The best metaphor to explain this is a package of sliced own-label sausage from your supermarket.

The label may say "top quality" or "premium" but in reality, it's just compressed waste meat and everyone knows it.

If you are self-taught or studying at a less established art school, or if you're just starting out and don't have a very keen eye for art, it can be easy to make mistakes. Therefore, for the time being, orient yourself only to absolutely established museums. Only this is art. Ignore everything else. Once you have developed an understanding of art, you can include established galleries, and then add more and more.

It is amazing how many people, even some longtime players in the art world, have no idea about the artistic canon. So don't let yourself be misled.

1.2. The artist

Whether you call yourself an artist or not is up to you. "Artist" is not a protected professional title. Whether others perceive you as an artist depends largely on whether your output is classified as part of the artistic canon and is recognized as art by society.

Traditionally, artists are seen as the sum of their idea-generating creativity and their consummate handcraft. But if you look at Jeff Koons today, for example, he is really just an idea generator and workshop manager. But that's not to be underestimated, because running a workshop can be much more complex than doing handcraft on your own. In the workshop, work and sometimes creativity is distributed among a team. Many people think this is a new concept, forgetting Andy Warhol, who produced art in his "factories" like on an assembly line (and – what's more – defined an artist cult that is still influential today).

We can even go much further back: As early as the Renaissance or in the Baroque period, there were workshops and joint works, as for example with Rembrandt. The idea and the commission went through the master, while the work was often completed as a team. Here, it should be mentioned that at that time, almost all commissions came from the church, the state, or the elites.

The art world today is larger and more complex than ever. If you want to survive here, you need more than a little creativity and handcraft. Some people like to talk about talent. But what does talent entail? Does it also mean you have a strong will and great perseverance? Because both are definitely necessary if you want to exist as an independent artist in the art system.

Anyone who sees artistic work as a profession and approaches it accordingly in a professional manner has already taken a big step in the right direction.

1.3. Success

Basically, you define what success means to you, but in real life, the measures of a successful career as an artist are recognition and money. However, there are different definitions of success in the art world, too. For example, there is not only one league in which you can become a champion, but several.

Even if you are successful in some ways, that is no guarantee of satisfaction or self-fulfillment. This may be because you have been disappointed by reality, your interests have changed, or you have run out of energy or passion over the years. You have to figure that out for yourself.

"Success requires a lot of sacrifices. The biggest of these is time."

The conditions for an artist to be successful are better today than ever before: We are living in a golden age for artists. Never before in history have there been so many artists, art collectors, and institutions showing and promoting art. In 2019, the global art market revenue exceeded $64 billion. In addition, several billion dollars in funding from private and public sources benefit artists directly and indirectly. It has probably never been easier to become successful.

2. The system

The art world is a bit like the soccer world. Before you can play, you have to know the game. What does the playing field look like? What are the basic rules of the game? What are the common rules of conduct? Besides the players on the field, are there other players such as coaches, referees, sponsors, and so on?

It is the same in art. If you want to play, you must first get to know the system and how it works. In the following chapter, an attempt is made to explain the art system. Not everything contained in this chapter is charming. However, much of it is considered common practice today, so it is therefore relevant and can be seen as a set of unwritten rules.

Don't get hung up on rules that you don't want to accept because they seem unfair or unappealing. But feel free to make a resolution to change them if you ever have the chance later.

2.1. Players and terms

Art is created by the artist, but it only manifests itself through the interaction of the individual players in the art system. In the following, an attempt is made to introduce the relevant players of the art system and clarify some terms. Of course, the boundaries are not always as clearly drawn as is presented here for ease of understanding.

"For a gallery, a work has to be sellable. For a museum, its content has to be exciting."

First and foremost, we need to distinguish between two types of artist: One type is more market-oriented – let's call them **"market artists"** – and the other type tends to serve museums and major exhibitions, such as the biennales, so let's call them **"biennale artists"** here. Market artists are usually characterized by their production of art that is easier to interpret and more marketable, and attracts the interest of galleries early on. Their career plan is to live off the sales of their art production and, if possible, to continuously increase their prices. As for biennale

21

artists: Their works often go beyond the constraints of a conventional gallery in terms of form and complexity alone. And in many cases, only the mediation of art, which is standard in a museum, makes it possible to grasp the work in its entirety. Here, the focus is more on the content of the work and less on the formal implementation. At the same time, works by biennale artists are more difficult to sell, because they can be large and bulky, are less likely to follow aesthetic rules, are conceptually based, and so on. Biennale artists survive, at least at the beginning of their careers, primarily thanks to private and government funding. Nowadays, it is a fact that biennale artists are strongly intertwined with the art market, although not everyone likes to hear that. Usually, of course, the boundaries blur as the artist becomes more successful. Nevertheless, this categorization and the questions that follow from it – which all artists must ask themselves – are very helpful in understanding the art system and making proper use of it.

Below is a list of key players and terms in the art system to aid your further understanding.

Art production
(The artist, the artist's employees, suppliers, and specialized art production companies)

Artists produce their art. They can do this independently, delegate it to employees in their studio, or have the manufacturing work outsourced to external service providers. Often, it is a mixture of all the above options. In recent years, art production companies have specialized in the complete realization of works of art. In extreme cases, the artist only supplies the idea. The realization and sometimes also the installation at the exhibition site is done entirely by the art production company.

Education
(Art schools, postgraduate programs)

Over the last hundred years, art schools have established themselves as optimal training centers for artists. They are completely integrated into today's art system and offer the best starting opportunities for a successful career as an artist. They can be organized privately or by the state.

Their reputation precedes them in each case and it is easy to distinguish between good and bad art schools. However, much also depends on individual student preferences.

Postgraduate programs, as defined here, are programs offered by a few institutions. They are often a combination of residency and study and last several years. They are aimed at ambitious, aspiring artists (usually after their studies) and can sometimes be pioneering in nature (examples include the Rijksakademie and the Royal Academy). Often, academic titles are not awarded on such programs.

In addition, there are private organizations that offer courses in the field of art, often limiting themselves to teaching individual techniques. These are, however, mainly of value to amateur artists.

Funding for artists
(Art prizes/awards, grants, scholarships, fellowships, stipends, artist-in-residence programs (residencies), patrons)

Art prizes/awards give you money, but they also usually give you a platform via the associated exhibition. Work stipends, for example, cover your fixed costs for housing, food, and materials by paying a monthly amount for a certain period of time. Artist-in-residence programs are residencies that sometimes include work stipends and are often abroad. They allow you to work in a protected environment and to network and be inspired in new, exciting places. The awarded funding is an important form of validation and recognition of your art and thus paves the way for you to position yourself successfully as an artist. It is often the basis for further awards and recognition. Patrons buy works from you in the early stages, and support you financially and through their connections.

Bringing art to the public
(Galleries, museums, kunsthalles, collections, alternative spaces – that is, artist-run spaces, artists' cooperative galleries, project spaces – major exhibitions such as biennales, and so on)

Galleries are listed here only for the sake of completeness. They are explained under "dealing."

The use of the terms "museum, kunsthalle, collection" varies as much from case to case as the institutions themselves and the terms can therefore not always be clearly separated. Together, they are among the most important institutions in the art system. Some of them have their own collection, some have a governing association or foundation, others have a supporters/friends association, some are organized by the state, others are private, and others still are private but receive additional state funding. If they are state-run, they usually have an educational function. If they have their own collection, the state, the foundation, or the supporters/friends association can provide annual funding, for example, to enhance the collection through targeted acquisitions or to have the local art scene represented as a basic principle. In addition to their own exhibits, they often manage and preserve permanent loans from private collections, comprising individual works or entire collections. The number of private institutions has grown enormously in recent years. All of these institutions are instrumental in building an artist's reputation, such as through exhibitions, catalog publications, acquisitions for their own collections, and so on.

The term alternative spaces is used here to refer to all "small" exhibition spaces that are neither classic galleries nor any of the previously mentioned institutions. Often organized by artists themselves, they are frequently the first port of call for artists to gain an insight into the exhibition business – and sometimes they can become very influential. They range from non-commercial experimental spaces to established artists' cooperative galleries that are financed through the sale of works.

Major exhibitions such as the Venice Biennale or the documenta in Kassel are the absolute yardsticks of the art world and are unparalleled shows. They are the antithesis of the art market, with which they are nevertheless intertwined. Regarding the name "biennale," it should be noted that this is not a protected term, but it is simply the name given to an event that takes place every two years. The first art biennale was in Venice in 1895, and the second was the São Paulo Biennale in 1951. Biennales have mushroomed, especially in the last few decades. The seal of quality originally associated with the name "biennale" should therefore be treated with caution.

Positioning
(Curators, critics, art historians and academics, literature, trade press, the press, social media)

Curators select one or more artists and put the works together in an exhibition and a common context. They either work on a freelance basis or are affiliated with an institution.

Critics evaluate art and position it in the artistic canon. This is mainly done in the form of a text that is published in some way. If art critics express themselves about an artist, whether positively or negatively, this is nowadays always beneficial for the artist's career due to the attention it attracts. Nevertheless, the influence of art criticism in general has, in fact, tended to diminish compared with the past.

Ideally, art historians and academics evaluate and position art primarily objectively. They are active wherever an academic view of art is required. Possible jobs are, for example, as a head of a museum or in the conservational management of a collection or at an auction house, but jobs as curators or gallery employees are also common.

Literature includes books and catalogs. The mention of an artist in literature is important evidence of his or her relevance in the art world.

The trade press and the general press, both printed and digital, are the seismographs of the art world – and are accordingly relevant for an artist's career.

Social media is no less relevant in the art system. Expert reception can also happen through social media. Sometimes, however, the dissemination of a posting is not in proportion to its relevance. A distorted picture can therefore emerge.

Dealing
(Galleries, art dealers, art fairs, art auctions, art advisors, art flippers)

Today, galleries are the most well-known places where art is sold. Exhibitions are organized on a gallery's own premises. Often, they have a fixed circle of artists they represent and with whom they collaborate over several years. Galleries give artists attention and a certain validity, and can provide them with an income. Ideally, they both grow together.

Art dealers, unlike gallery owners, do not operate an exhibition space. They have no intrinsic attachment to artists. They are opportunists who broker individual paintings and groups of works between sellers and buyers. They travel a lot and are constantly on the phone.

Art fairs are the global hubs of the art trade; they usually last only a few days and have developed into a showcase for seeing and being seen in the art world. They have popped up everywhere in recent years. The five most important and largest fairs are currently (as at 2019) Art Basel (Basel, Miami, Hong Kong), The Armory Show (New York), FIAC (Paris), Art Cologne (Cologne), and Frieze (London, New York, Los Angeles).

Art auctions are arguably the most influential institutions in the secondary art market. "Secondary art market" means that the work has usually already been sold to a collector through a gallery before. The collector now offers it for sale again, hoping to get a higher price than when he or she bought it. The price increase achieved here is one of the most important drivers of an artist's career in the market. Accordingly, a decline in the market prices achieved by an artist can be cataclysmic.

Art advisors, also known as art consultants, advise art buyers in making decisions about purchases of works. They see themselves as art experts. Their clients are primarily individuals and institutions, whom they assist in the long-term management of an art collection. Assignments commissioned by clients range from capital growth to building a thematic collection. Art advisors are either independent or part of an institution, such as a bank.

Art flippers and art flipping are terms that appeared only after the turn of the millennium. Art flippers buy one or more works and then resell them. Art dealers do the same thing and so it's basically nothing new. Rather, the word stands for a trend, but also clearly sets new benchmarks. Some people insinuate that art flippers often have little – or very market-specific – knowledge of art. Art flippers' clients are also mainly interested only in the increase in value of the works. Ethical and moral principles in the art market are generally a matter of contention, but art flippers are accused of having the fewest principles of all and pursuing only financial goals. Buying and selling takes place in very short succession. The profits achieved are sometimes immense.

The works are selected solely on the basis of their marketability. The actual artists and their œuvres are of minimal significance.

Art buyers
(Collectors)

Art buyers buy art for various reasons and with varying regularity. The motivations range from prestige and decoration to investment, tax optimization, and money laundering. Buyers can be individuals, companies, and public and private institutions. Anyone who intentionally and regularly buys art can be called a collector.

2.2. The different leagues of the art world

In which league do you want to play?

International artist
Premier league, the elite league: You are represented by at least one important international gallery or several important national galleries in different countries and in international museums with solo exhibitions.

National artist
You are represented at a major national gallery and in national museums with solo exhibitions. Here, it is important to distinguish whether your country is one of the global players in the arts or not. Depending on where you are an artist, proximity to the class of the international artist will vary.

Regional artist
You are locally known and respected, have regular exhibitions, and may even be featured in a group show at a nationally known institution.

Amateur artist

Amateur artists are probably the happiest artists of all those listed. You are passionate, interested, and work regularly. Here and there, you display your work at regional exhibitions.

Niche artist

And then there is the niche artist. In your field, you can be anything between regionally and internationally known, and your earnings can be between nothing and lots of money. Some see you as an artist, some see you as an amateur artist, and some see you as being outside the art world. Examples include artists from the field of street art/urban art, erotic art, maritime painting, and so on.

Only the top class guarantees that you can earn money with art. It is also possible in other leagues to make a living from art, but it is not self-evident.

There are, in fact, also amateur artists who earn a lot of money with their art. They also see themselves as professional artists, but in the art world, unfortunately, they are completely insignificant. Just as a reminder: This book is oriented toward the general artistic canon and it pursues a path with the goal of getting into the premier league.

Let us make clear here: 80–90% of all artists are not suited to becoming successful in the premier league of art. The league you can play in depends on how successfully you can establish yourself in the art system. Not everyone is suitable for every league, and advancement through the leagues cannot be achieved through hard work alone.

Note that as a regional artist, for example, you are subject to different laws and rules than an international artist. Here, it is less important that you are internationally known, but rather that you are well connected in your region, that you are – in some cases – satisfy the regional demands in terms of content and aesthetics, and that you are perhaps active in local institutions in order to develop and expand your reputation on the local art scene. Where you are rooted, you serve your clientele, most of whom are personally known and familiar to you.

2.3. Mechanisms in the art system

It is not easy to see through the mechanisms of the art system and it is always only a snapshot, because the system is constantly changing. This chapter is designed to sharpen your focus, so that you can independently seek out new and different mechanisms in the future.

The evaluation of art

"Art is what is in a museum."

Apart from the often negligible material value, art has no real value. The artist, as part of the art system, creates the work along with its content and thus gives it value for the first time in the sense of it being art. The subsequent formation of value occurs in the context of the past and present of art and the art system. The work of art is then given additional value by further players in the system. To put it simply: The value of a work of art is the sum of all the layers of value from the individual players.

If artists are invited by a curator to exhibit at an established museum, their rating usually increases, and so does their work. If an art critic writes an article about the exhibition in an art magazine, the exhibition gains more attention. Accordingly, the status of the artist involved grows, and so does the value in most cases.
If a painting from a private collection is exhibited in a well-known museum, the value of the painting usually increases.
The art system is always connected to the society of the time. If its values change, this can also have an effect on the evaluation of art. Art of the past is therefore also constantly reinterpreted. Basically, you can only judge art if you know and take into account the underlying art system.

The dependencies of the players

You have already learned: The players collectively give a work of art or an artist value or recognition. However, several players are always necessary to create value; value creation cannot be achieved by one player alone. The various players in the art system are thus interdependent and their careers or successes closely interlinked. If an artist becomes successfully established, the entire value chain can benefit. All the players who have worked with that artist can then gain prestige and, in some cases, turn the artist's success to their advantage or capitalize on it – even if they are not directly responsible for the further success of the artist.

Art as a status symbol and an investment

Art has always been a status symbol, but in times of low interest rates and after the elimination of some tax havens, it has also become a common form of investment. This circumstance has had an enormous impact on the art system and the assessment of art. The changes this has triggered in the art system are much more far-reaching than you might think at first glance. The globalization of the art market and the unprecedented influx of capital with absurdly high auction prices that perplex the public are only the tip of an iceberg of effects.

Movements and the formation of terms

There are trends in art. And these trends can spring from many sources. They can arise organically from art, be socially induced, and sometimes be politically motivated. Trends can condense into movements. If they are substantial, last for a long time, and/or a lively discourse takes place, they can find their way into art history as terms.

The works or exhibitions related to these trends and currents are characterized by similar formal language and/or thought.

Examples of movements are: Impressionism, Dadaism, Pop Art, Arte Povera, and, from more recent times, Postcolonialism.

Discovery and exclusivity

In the art world, people like to boast about discoveries and exclusivity. Curators are often looking for artists who have never been shown in their region, or who have only been shown in less influential institutions than the host's, or haven't been shown for a long time. All curators want to be the first in their region to exhibit the great and emerging artist. But this is not only true in the exhibition business; collectors don't want to be the last to buy a work by an artist who is currently in vogue, either. Trends in the art world often work similarly to new trends in the fashion/consumer world. Some things quickly become must-haves and you can make a name for yourself with them.

Résumé and career progression

Artists' résumés have become enormously important. Their career progression now depends greatly on their art school's reputation, residencies/awards, participation in exhibitions, and so on. Often one leads to the other. If an artist has been selected for a well-known residency, his or her chances of being invited to a major exhibition later are much higher. Juries have to look through a lot of applications in a short time, so they often pre-sort based on the résumé. Also, juries tend not to take risks and it is only logical for them to highly rate those who already have achievements.

Success attracts success

If an artist receives increased attention, be it through an art award or a magazine article, for example, then he or she automatically becomes interesting for those people (curators, gallery owners, and so on) who need "fresh talents," and who prepare them and then present them as their new discovery. It only seems understandable that they would jump on the bandwagon and help it gain speed through their engagement.

Quotas

Quotas (for example, the number of women/men) in exhibition participation, art prizes, and so on, are a fact of life today. Political correctness is becoming more and more established and various quotas (LGBTQ+, minority ethnic background, ethnicity, skin color, and so on) are now in place.

No one disputes that quotas can be justified. However, neither should we ignore the fact that they bring with them new problems. What you need to learn for yourself as an artist is to use quotas in your favor when and wherever you can.

Nepotism and "la famiglia"

"If you visit several art fairs and major exhibitions in one or two years, you'll find that it's often the same people you run into. The art world is surprisingly small. It's kind of a big family."

Nepotism is an integral and important part of the art system. The art system comprises many small circles that legitimize each other and maintain a close friendship. To put it simply: Most of it works through connections. A gallery exhibits you because someone recommended you, the gallery owner knows a curator who puts you in an exhibition, and so on.

But it goes even further than many think. A whole book could be written about it. You can call it "la famiglia" or simply see it as a win-win principle in the name of art. Here are two examples:

First, the Venice Biennale, an exhibition that takes place every two years and apparently focuses on current trends in global art, far removed from the art market. That's far from the truth. Renowned galleries provide huge sums of money and as a "thank you," their artists are shown at the Biennale. Sometimes, an artist's portfolio is made fit for the Biennale in advance. Works can be purchased by interested parties similar to an art fair. An extensive hospitality program for the galleries' regular customers rounds out their Venice visit.

It is not uncommon for public museums to receive works as gifts or on permanent loan. As a "thank you," these works, as well as others, are included in exhibitions. The artworks themselves also have a kind of résumé, and their career progression is referred to as provenance. If a work enters a collection or is exhibited in a museum, an entry is made in the provenance register, usually followed by an increase in value.

2.4. Other influences

The art system does not exist in a vacuum and should never be considered in isolation. Many things influence it, sometimes more directly and sometimes more indirectly. Exploring all possible influences – such as technical progress, globalization, and so on – would go beyond the scope of the chapter, but we will look at two influential topics in brief.

The economy

The economic situation, globally but also in individual parts of the world, always has a decisive influence on the art system. Collectors, for example, earn their money mainly in the private sector and use it later to buy art. If collectors' main source of income falls, they can buy less art. The budget for art and culture of states, institutional collections and their sponsors is always linked to the economic situation. Consequently, the art market is interconnected with other markets. And thus, during an economic crisis, there is generally much less buying on the art market and much less support of the arts.

Also, works may come onto the market unexpectedly from bankrupted collectors, and the market may not be able to absorb them. This may result in a drop in the price of individual artists.

It is not only artists or the other previously mentioned players who are dependent on the economic situation. The art system has become a huge global industry. The list is long. It starts with the stores for artists' materials and also includes transport and insurance companies, exhibition builders, specialized companies, and so on. And it provides jobs for millions of people in galleries, museums and other art institutions, publishing houses, as assistants to artists, and so on.

Politics

In many countries, art is funded by the state. Accordingly, politics has an impact on, for example, museums and art academies. This can happen through money, but also through a more targeted type of influence. The state can exert influence even on private art institutions, if only through the tax rate on art sales, which can have a major impact on the local art system.

Art is mostly subject to freedom of expression. This does not mean that art that criticizes a system cannot polarize, but in rare cases it leads to punishment or imprisonment.

Nevertheless, in some countries, art is censored or only art that is loyal to the state receives funding. In such places, art critical of the state can have drastic consequences, up to and including the death penalty.

Depending on where you live, you may benefit from favorable cultural policies – or you may have to watch your back.

If you come from a repressive country, you can move to a country with freedom of speech and from there use your art to protest against the conditions in your home country. This may change little, but can sometimes go down well in the art system of your host country.

3. Art – the reality check

"The bad news first: The art world is a utopia. The good news: If you become part of the system before you give up or go insane, life in this utopia is pretty good."

Are we being given the true picture of art? Is the concept of it purely wishful thinking and far from reality? The reality check is intended to give an idea of what art is today or how it is actually perceived in society beyond the usual definitions and how it influences society.

Art is often seen as the embodiment of the wonderful and free genius of humankind. Perhaps in the naive mind of many an artist it is, but in reality it has been in the service of faith, power, and wealth for thousands of years and has been instrumentalized for their purposes.

Art is a luxury

"Art is only bought by people whose refrigerator is full, whose car is safe in the garage, and whose city trip over Easter is already booked."

You can spin it any way you want, but art is and remains a luxury. Although art is bought by the middle classes upwards, the biggest sales market is clearly to be found in the upper class.
Luxury goods are one thing above all: status symbols. And so people use art to set themselves apart from the rest of society. But art is even more. Art is unsurpassed in its usefulness as a luxury good: It is not only a status symbol of wealth, but it also suggests intellect and worldliness, it is not perishable (with a few exceptions) and its value not infrequently increases significantly over time, so it has thus become a common type of investment.

Art events are no longer just for art, they have become a social showcase and a pleasure for the upper classes.

Even looking at art can sometimes become a luxury, considering the hours of waiting and the steep entrance fees at the Louvre or the Vatican, for example, but also at other museums and collections.

"To exaggerate: Art has become the hobby of the super-rich – and mega art events have become their amusement parks."

"The rich have a lot of money and like to buy art. You can profit from that."

Art is elitist

"You think you're a genius and you think you're helping society – but society doesn't even notice you anymore. Because it can't relate to art."

Contemporary art is created in a closed system by a few and interpreted by just as few. Art does not claim to be universally understandable and accessible. In other words, even if we could assume that art in the form of images is available to everyone via the Internet, this does not mean that everyone would understand it. It often requires additional knowledge through education or on-site experience in order to understand the work, which not everyone can afford due to lack of money or time.

Furthermore, many people do not have the courage to go to museums or galleries or engage with art.

Art is hypocritical

Contemporary art likes to show off by addressing political topics and exposing and coming to grips with current and historical events or the wrongs of the world. This is fundamentally something to be approved of, but far from all of it is meant as seriously as would seem. Rather, some artists follow a currently prevailing trend and thereby hope to attract attention in the art system and beyond. A lot of political art also follows social trends and does not formulate its own opinion.

"Art as a political message: How often has art actually started a discussion or made changes?"

"Also questionable are the artists who are part of the art system and loudly rail against capitalism."

Art displaces people

Few people want to admit that artists' studios, exhibition spaces, galleries, and museums are an important driver of gentrification. In various cities, it has been found that they are largely responsible for the fact that rents are rising.

Due to a lack of money, artists are often the first to settle in cheap neighborhoods that are sometimes struggling with crime or vacant properties, setting a process of gentrification in motion. Exhibition spaces, more hip people, bars, and galleries quickly follow – as do higher rents.

In some major cities, both in Europe and America, even isolated protests by citizens and politicians have recently turned against exhibition spaces and galleries and successfully prevented them from opening. In some places, the art scene has pushed so much away that it has actually pushed itself away.

Art for the warehouse

Most art does not hang on the walls of museums or collectors, but is packed in boxes and stored in warehouses. Art is mainly purchased by a few thousand art collections privately or institutionally. If you're lucky, once the box reaches the buyer, it will be opened and a report will be written about the art work's condition by a responsible party. The actual owner often doesn't even look at the work. And then it ends up in storage, often for a long time.

There are cases where the works are simply packed into air-conditioned shipping containers. The containers are then stacked somewhere in the middle of nowhere in a run-down warehouse.

In extreme cases, the works are even locked up in a bonded warehouse (freeport). Here they are stored for the purpose of avoiding import taxes and, if they change hands, only the name needs to be changed in the warehouse management database. Some of these works will probably never see the light of day again.

Art attracts dubious business dealings

What do you do, for example, if you have piles of dirty money? Swiss banks don't want it any more. If you buy a Ferrari, it's obvious that you spent two or three hundred thousand dollars on it. Here, art is much more discreet and does not make you appear boastful. Rather, it is considered fashionable to promote and collect art. Maybe you discovered the artist very early and bought the paintings for peanuts – who knows? Basically, you will not be asked as many questions during the purchasing process. Also, no one is surprised by large amounts of cash. Cash payment is still common in this sector.

And let's be honest: New galleries and young artists only just get by. Rarely does anyone ask where the money comes from.

Large sums of money can be parked easily. And compared to money in a bank account or other investment, art can prove to be very manageable, crossing national borders in simple and sometimes difficult-to-trace ways.

Since works of art are often unique pieces of which there are necessarily only one, their valuation can be strongly subjective and even an enormous increase in value in a short time is nothing abnormal. However, such increases in value can also be faked and misused for money laundering purposes.

Art attracts speculators

"The modern art system is a fruit of global capitalism."

Over the past 30 years, speculation in the financial markets has faced increasingly tough times. It is not that speculation itself has decreased, but rather that the regulations have become stricter and the penalties harsher. Maybe this is a reason for increased speculation in the art market? Whatever, the fact is that there is no regulation in this sector, making the art market a paradise for speculators. If, in the financial world, the mention of the term "insider trading" prompts a visit from the police, the same term in the art world gets the party started with champagne.

And so, in recent years, a business has developed in which you can ask yourself whether art has any further meaning at all, other than for speculation.

4. The life of an artist

"The life of an artist is tough but also ultra-awesome. Yes, you can get up at eleven in the morning, open a bottle of wine and celebrate life."

As an artist, you are the freest member of the entire art value chain. You have lower initial costs than the gallery owner, you're likely more creative than the curator, and you have more flexible hours than the art academic or historian. And, last but not least, you can allow yourself even more quirks without running the risk of not being taken seriously. But, on the other hand, it is probably the most difficult task. You always have to motivate yourself and you're the one who has to work the hardest on your own to achieve anything. The others can select, regulate, contextualize, and sell what exists; you have to create.

"How does an artist's life begin? It doesn't start with the first exhibition or the first day at art school. It starts in your head."

If you want to become a hairdresser, for example, you usually do an apprenticeship in hairdressing. This lasts about three years and requires 100% of your attention. And here the artist differs only slightly. Being an artist is a profession that you have to learn over several years and that also requires 100% of your attention. But your life as an artist doesn't cease when you close your studio door behind you. And even with your death, your life as an artist ends, but the career of your art doesn't. Art as a sideline doesn't work.

We often hear the complaint that self-exploitation is rampant in the art world. As an artist, you're usually a one-person show. You will take a major part of your most important career steps on your own and you will bear the responsibility. An extreme use of all your energy is required, similar to top-class athletes. Whether you want to call that self-exploitation is up to you. The fact is that it is practically impossible to become successful without extreme dedication. Remember: You're also the one who gets the credit in the end. In the end, it's your name under the artwork that hangs at MoMA, not that of all the people who enabled you to get there.

It should be made clear here that the following chapters are aimed at professional artists and those who want to become one. It is assumed that as an artist you are willing to dedicate 100% of your life to art from now on.

4.1. Basic requirements

The following three basic requirements are essential for a career as an artist.

Time

"Success doesn't come from 'easy' but from 'goal-oriented.'"

At the beginning of your artistic career, think about how many years you want to invest in starting your career as an artist. And let us say right away: If you're thinking of investing anything less than five years "full time," don't even bother starting. And after ten years, statistically speaking, the chances of a breakthrough don't get bigger, but tend to get smaller. This is mainly due to the fact that you have not used your time effectively, or, most likely, approached your art career with too little commitment and planning.

Money

"If you know how to manage your money, you have a clear advantage."

It's now clear that the beginning of an artist's career takes a lot of time. Accordingly, the cost of simply living consumes an enormous amount of money. $60,000 is the minimum you have to calculate – and there is basically no upper limit.

You should think about how you're going to finance that beforehand. Will your family help you? Are there any state or private scholarships or funding available? Even if you become one of the few artists who can make money from their art, it will take several years to reach that point. Most likely, you will have to work in other fields on the side – as a "day job" – and tighten your belt pretty darn tight.

If you depend on a part-time job to make a living, use your qualifications and either do something where you earn good money or look for a job in the art scene (gallery, museum, auction house, and so on) where you can gain experience and contacts in the art system that will then be useful for your career.

Many artists are not good with money, especially when they have some. Learn to manage money effectively! Money is one of the most important factors that determine the rise and fall of an artist's career. Only if you use all your resources optimally and efficiently, can you become successful.

So, sit down and analyze your monthly expenses. What are your biggest outgoings? Can anything be optimized? And where else does your money go? In canvas and paint? Or into your dealer's pocket? Or the daily Coca-Cola from the kiosk? Experience shows that you save the most money if you carefully consider all amounts under $10. Learn where you are spending your money pointlessly. How much money do you spend each month in the name of art? For materials, tools, museum visits, and so on? Your money must be invested in art. Or, if your art doesn't need money, reduce the hours you work in your day job. Live the lifestyle that fits your budget, not that of your hipster buddies from university.

"Many people reward themselves with a piece of cake, a trip to the cinema, a new dress, and so on. You are an artist, reward yourself with a new paintbrush or canvas."

Work

"Most artists don't make it because they're stupid, lazy, selfish, or not focused on their goals."

Write down as a number how many hours per week you can work on your art. If the number is less than 17, then you should give up right now. However, we are talking about the bare minimum here, which will only be enough to establish you as an artist in exceptional cases. The more time you put into your work, the greater your chances of success usually are. Don't get false impressions, though: If you make it as an artist, expect to work between 40 and 60 hours a week.

And don't forget that you should also visit exhibitions and network with others regularly.

Make yourself a weekly schedule, like you used to have in school: Write down which days you work in your day job for money, what times you are in the studio, and so on. Also enter your leisure or relaxation time in the weekly schedule. This is helpful for many people to draw a line between themselves and work.

4.2. Your microcosm

To become successful, you need to build your own little art system over the course of your career. Start this as soon as you decide to pursue a career as an artist. The basis of this is the sum of all your social contacts since you were born. Through studying, networking, and so on, many more contacts are added over time. All your friends are potential guests at your first exhibition. You sell your first paintings to your relatives, organize your first exhibition with your fellow students, ask your professor in college for your first letter of recommendation for an art award.

Grow with your generation. Cultivate your contacts. Make friends. Swap ideas. Support each other. Friends of yours may become important artists, curators, gallery owners, or collectors. They can open doors for you later. Today, you can recommend a friend for an exhibition, while next time, another friend will invite you to exhibit. What goes around, comes around.

It's not only about individuals helping you in a tangible way, it's also about them making you appear professional. In other words, it's about recognition and legitimation. For example, if you have an established curator in your circle of friends, this subconsciously confirms that you are an exciting artist.

He who sows, reaps. At some point, you realize how one contact leads to the next, and many things become easier. Your contacts – your microcosm – are essential to a successful career as an artist.

4.3. Career planning

"A career is like an apple tree, it needs time and care. You have to wait years for the first harvest."

Think about where you want to go and how you can get there. To do this, study the résumés of other artists. What did they do and when? From the career analysis of young, up-and-coming artists, you can also find out which cities, collectors, institutions, residencies, and awards are in vogue right now. Exchange ideas with artist friends, discuss with them how they plan their careers. And then make your own plan for your career as an artist. Set goals and define milestones. The plan is designed to help you stay on track with your goals and set parameters to guide you.

This plan is your tool for self-control. Refer to it regularly and check how diligent and determined you are. You can also adjust the plan at any time. Life changes quickly. But do not deceive yourself. You don't need to be in a desperate hurry, because your art needs time to mature, your personality needs to be allowed to develop, and so does your network. Knowledge and experience must be accumulated, but do not waste time. You can quickly get caught in endless loops – and valuable months, even years, pass you by without being used.

"All of a sudden, five years have gone by and you don't know how it happened."

Personal dreams no longer have a place if they can't be connected to your work or constitute more than a "vacation" to give you a well-deserved break and bring inspiration.

Gaining experience outside the art world can be very enriching and helpful. It gives you the opportunity to learn skills in a hands-on way. Besides that, it gives you a glimpse into the real world and can also serve as an anchor. You lose touch with reality in the art world faster than you think. But basically, you should have had these experiences before your career as an artist. If they are part of your absolutely necessary part-time job, don't lose sight of your career as an artist.

The 35-year limit

If you don't manage to achieve significant success and become relevant in the art system before you turn 35, it will be much, much more difficult to make the breakthrough afterwards. After 35 at the latest, you are no longer considered a young artist, and many major grants exclude applicants who are older than 30 or 35.

The myth of "live fast, die young"

Artists such as Jean-Michel Basquiat, Martin Kippenberger, and Dash Snow lived short and excessive lives and thus went down in history. Such journeys through life were possible in the past, but whether they still are today is questionable. In fact, they were exceptions even then, and the chances of being left behind are still huge. It is very important to say here that you must already be very successful and well-known during your lifetime. Your breakthrough will not come posthumously.

"Don't forget, after the countless depraved drinking orgies, the crassest drug parties, and partying till you drop, something has to be accomplished, too. The vomit on the canvas won't be enough to give you your breakthrough."

4.4. Choosing the right location

Not every location offers you equally good opportunities to connect with the art world. At the beginning of the 20th century, Paris was practically the only metropolis with a vibrant and concentrated young art scene – and so it was an easy decision where to go as a young artist. But today there are several trend-setting cities that provide a good base. The undisputed number one for several decades is New York, likely followed by London. But there are also many other cities that offer a good entry into the art system – and they can often be much less expensive. However, your chance of success is clearly reduced if you get stuck there.

The artist city of Berlin is a long way from the leaders New York and London, but it currently boasts the best value for money. As a result, it has established itself as – and remains – the most cost-effective alternative and exciting melting pot for the art system.

First, decide on a prestigious art school, no matter where it is located. In fact, there are a few tremendously good art schools in regions that, apart from the well-connected university itself, otherwise have no functioning art system or a very insignificant one. Leave these regions before you graduate, or at the latest immediately afterwards.

Go where all the other artists are. Some artists make the mistake of wanting to avoid places with many artists in order to avoid competition. Two comments on this: First, just because there are many artists in one city doesn't mean they all work hard. It is proven, for example, that the lower the cost of living, the less hardworking the artists. Second, if you're not confident you can compete, it's better to give up now.

What is good for the beginning is not necessarily good for your later career. Changes of location are imperative in your career as an artist.
Keep an eye out for where young talent is being discovered today. Regions are shaped to a great extent by art schools, institutions, galleries, and collectors. Where are the optimal conditions for the current stage of your career? Is the state involved in creating good conditions for artists here? In addition, there are important funding awards and exhibitions that are limited exclusively to artists (residing or working) in a region. These can be very prestigious, and can represent the next leap in your career.

You might think that the Internet has made the importance of the right location obsolete, but that is too simplistic: A trendy location gives you optimal conditions for networking and developing a professional image, and makes you more interesting overall.

Conclusion: On the one hand, in New York the cost of living is about three times higher than in an average art metropolis, but on the other hand, you have a three-times-greater chance of becoming successful if you move there.

"So, if you have rich parents, put yourself in pole position and go to New York!"

4.5. Studies

Studying at an accredited art school is absolutely essential today. Its primary purpose is to give you an understanding of art and to learn to critically examine and position your own artistic work, as well as to build your own network. All these points are absolutely central to your career as an artist. Of course, art school offers you even more, for example, a platform to try yourself out, a cheap workplace or access to expertise and workshops. But, in fact, you also need mandatory proof of attendance at an art school, preferably with a degree. As mentioned earlier, an artist's résumé has become incredibly important and you can rest assured that it has become virtually impossible to have a successful career as an artist without studying art. You just have to accept that. In principle, it would be possible to achieve everything without doing any studying, but the effort would be many times more and in the end you would still not have any proof of attendance at art school.

Choice of art school and application

Your career as an artist begins at the latest with the choice of the right art school. The more prestigious your art school is, the greater your chance of success later. However, this also usually means that it is proportionately harder to get a place there and fees are correspondingly higher. The art schools that give students the greatest chance of success are probably in New York and London at the moment. However, this does not mean that the most expensive art school is automatically the right one for you. You also need to fit into the art school. You must be able to keep pace with the language, the direction, the pressure, the lifestyle, the costs, and so on. If your budget is limited, some schools will be out of the question. If you have a fixed area of interest, it should also play a role in your choice of art school.

It's important that your professor can make sense of your art. He or she needs to understand what's on your mind and be able to talk to you about it. But your fellow students also play a significant role in your artistic development. They too should have an understanding of you as a person and, ideally, your art. It is therefore important that you are placed in a class where you feel comfortable. This does not mean that the professor or fellow students must necessarily think your work is good, but the conditions must be met for a constructive discourse to take place that will foster your development.

Typically, an art school has various, usually renowned artists as professors who teach and/or mentor students in a whole range of different and conceivable ways. Lectures, seminars, group meetings, one-to-one discussions, workshops, projects, and so on – all these things can happen in lecture halls, studios, and workshops, but also outside the art school building. The regularity of events can vary from daily to six-monthly.
In addition, there are often a number of other professors and lecturers, such as art historians, philosophers, and so on, who give theoretical lectures or seminars and organize workshops. Furthermore, there are workshops and labs where you can gain practical knowledge. These are often led by former students or experts from various (outside) fields, many of whom are active as artists.

Each university has different professors and thus different areas of focus and interest. Some art schools and countries prefer a more conceptual approach to the study of art, while others take a more craft-based approach.

Generally, artists rarely say that they were very unhappy with their choice of art school. If, however, some of them had pulled themselves together, crossed national borders, or extracted more money from their parents in order to study at a school with a better reputation, they might be famous today.

You should also be aware that, in certain countries and at certain state universities, courses of study are free for foreign students, too, or are limited to the usual $200 to $1,000 course fees per semester that everyone must pay.

For art schools, you must apply with a portfolio of work. On average, only between 5% and 20% of applicants are admitted after a thorough examination.

The art world is all about connections, and in the remotest sense that starts with the art school application process. If you want to increase your chances, consult the school, professors, students, and former students, and get more detailed information about preferences in application portfolios before you apply. Make yourself popular and seek contact.

If you don't succeed with your first application (which, by the way, is not uncommon) try a second and third time. Apply to another art school. Apply to several art schools at the same time.

"If you really want it, you can do it. You just need to get it together!"

Note: Art schools usually have university status, which means they generally require a high-school diploma, A-levels, or a general qualification for university entrance. At many art schools, however, it is possible in exceptional cases – if talent worthy of support can be identified – to be admitted without a high-school diploma or equivalent. This is specific to art schools.

During the study program

Use your time at art school to experiment artistically. Learn manual skills. Accumulate knowledge. Build a network – you'll need it later.

Degree

Bear in mind that graduating with an art-only degree will only help you if you want to pursue a career as an artist. Otherwise, it is more or less worthless.

The graduate exhibition should be your ticket to success. It is one of the most important moments in the early days of your career, where jurors, curators, gallery owners, and collectors can discover you. You should focus all your energies and pull out all the stops for this exhibition.

But success doesn't come automatically when you graduate. The fact is that only a few of the graduates are later able to establish themselves as successful artists.

"Graduation day comes for all graduates. In purely statistical terms, it is for many also the day on which their short careers as artists are buried."

Master's degree, Ph.D. and semester abroad

Many universities use the bachelor/master system, which means that after a bachelor's degree, you can still earn a master's degree. Certain schools even allow you to study for a Ph.D. in art. If you want to establish yourself as an artist, there is no good reason to study for a Ph.D. An additional master's degree is not generally recommended for everyone, either. Depending on your situation, you should decide for or against it. You should study for a master's degree at the same university as your bachelor's degree only in exceptional cases – for example, if you are already at a renowned school and have good contacts in its environment that need to be cultivated further. However, it should be noted that a master's degree at another university is a great way to grow your network, and if you earn it from a prestigious school abroad, it can give your résumé the boost it needs.

If you only aim to complete a bachelor's degree, it is recommended that you include at least one semester abroad toward the end of your course of study.

4.6. Partners and children

Let us state once again that the principle is: Everything for art.

Partners

By partner, we mean a husband, wife, boyfriend, girlfriend, or similar. Basically, your goal must be to invest maximum time and energy into your art. So, if you have the need for a partner, it is important that he or she does not hinder your creativity and career, but encourages you or even supports you. Partners can be important sources of inspiration, provide emotional balance and keep you grounded, but they can also rob you of time and energy that you then lack for your art. Here, you must make absolutely sure that the "costs" justify the "benefits." This may sound unromantic and mathematical at first, but an artist's work and life are often intertwined, and so your partner automatically exerts an influence on you and thus your being an artist. It is imperative that your partner has an understanding of you as an artist and takes you and your work 100% seriously. He or she must understand being an artist as a profession with all its duties and tasks. If this is not the case, sooner or later there will be tensions in your relationship that will distract you from your work.

A real-life example: It's Saturday and an important exhibition opening at the museum has been scheduled for the evening for a long time. You and your partner are spending a relaxing day at home and there are so many reasons not to go out in the evening. Will your partner motivate you to go out or stay home? Let's say you decide to go to the opening and your partner even goes with you, because you only plan to stay for just a little while. Now you get a surprise invitation to dinner from an important collector, right after the exhibition. Is it all too much for your partner? How do you decide? Do you go to dinner without him or her? Do you have to justify your decision later?

Use synergies. Find a partner who will not only accept you as an artist, but will help you move forward – or better still, you will help each other move forward. The romantic idea of the chaotic and creative artist and the partner who brings order into life is not so wrong, because both can benefit from each other. Also advantageous are partners who either have connections or know people with connections, and partners who are ambitious artists themselves or work in the art sector.

"A great combination is an artist with a wealthy partner who not only has the artist's back financially, but can also introduce him or her to high society."

Everyone needs their own dream. However, this does not exclude the possibility that both had the same dream before, or that the dreams complement each other wonderfully. It's bad when, in a relationship, only the dream of one of the two partners is made reality.

Experience shows that many artists waste their energy on the wrong choice of partner. Your choice of partner has a significant impact on your work and often on your career.

Finding the right partner is not easy. It may also be the case that the partner is not always the same throughout an artist's entire career. And not every partner is right for you at every stage of your career. Maybe you need some wild and uninhibited life experience first. A partner can give you the kick you need in the current stage of your career, but at the same time can prevent you from taking the next step. Partners tend to bind their counterpart to them out of their own interest, which can be a disaster for your career.

Therefore, recognize and take advantage of synergies and never lose focus on your art.

Children

Kids are great, but the chance of them thwarting your career is very high. This is not only the case with artists.

Countless great female artists have given up their careers because of a child. For some, the child was not the real reason, but rather the final act that had been coming for some time. Others were able to pick up their careers again later. For male artists, the situation is different, but it is similar: If they can transfer responsibility for the child to their partner, the child is less of a distraction. Whether the partner may agree and whether it is fair is, of course, another question.

The fact is that in many cases a child can be an enormous additional burden for artists – especially if money is tight or you don't have a partner who is happy to take on much of the responsibility. If you have not yet made the breakthrough and are still working solo, this extra workload can hinder your career.

Often it's about more than the time and attention that you have to spend on the child, because children also cost money. And then children often change the way their parents perceive things. If, in the past, you felt comfortable in a shaky financial situation for many years, you may suddenly feel the need to provide (long-term) security for your family. Parents fear that their child will become an outsider at school because all the other children are growing up in a supposedly protected environment. And suddenly the precarious artist's life is no longer compatible with family life.

We don't want you to get the wrong idea: Children are definitely an asset to an artist's life and there is nothing wrong with having children as an artist, but the conditions should be right, otherwise either your career or your family will suffer. For example, if you started your career early, put off having children, and planned well, there is a good chance you will have a happy family as an artist.

4.7. Responsibility

"If you want it easy, go to medical school."

As an artist, you are independent and responsible for yourself. So, you have to be far more responsible than an average employee, for example. An artist's hours are flexible and no one checks to see if you worked eight hours a day. As a rule, no one controls whether you work hard and are focused on your art and career.

This sounds like a small task, but it is an enormous challenge in many artists' lives. Distractions lurk everywhere. You don't get encouraged or reprimanded by your boss and you sometimes miss the relaxing conversations with colleagues during coffee breaks. You may have an exhibition planned in the distant future, which gives you a goal and keeps you on track – but often you're home alone with no goal, you have to force yourself to go to the studio and, once you're there, it doesn't mean that work will come naturally.

Sooner than you think, your art slips out of focus. Rest periods and inspiration are important, but at some point enough is enough. It's easy to lose yourself in your private sphere as an artist. After all, it's closely linked to your profession, in other words, your art.

You must learn to recognize dangers and deal with them. If you slip into a crisis, it is up to you to cope with it and overcome it.

Dangers and unnecessary distractions

Lack of respect for your working hours. If you're a surgeon, your parents aren't going to call you at work because their WiFi isn't working. If you're an artist, they may be tempted to do just that. Such an interruption pulls you out of work and, even if you are only on the phone for five minutes solving the problem, it breaks your chain of concentration and thoughts, and you may lose a whole hour or more. People have less respect for an artist's working hours. Be aware of this and don't be the always-available go-to person for the concerns of those around you.

The day job. Often, a day job or second job is necessary to meet the cost of living. Sometimes, you run the risk of getting lost in these jobs, if only because they are financially appealing. You can quickly get blown off course, simply because your focus in life shifts elsewhere.

Idleness. If life is sweet, temptations are many. For example, if your parents or the state are funding you or if you think you can afford to let yourself go a little, you may well take a liking to a certain lifestyle and neglect your work. As an artist, you don't have a boss breathing down your neck.

Digital time-wasters. Computers, cell phones, and televisions are great inventions with all sorts of uses, but they are also time drains. The Internet, the countless series available to stream, computer games, and social media can consume an unimaginable amount of your life, and afterwards you have achieved little or even – in most cases – nothing.

Don't get lost in a city or in its scene. You're new to a city, you settle in, and suddenly you feel at home. You know a lot of exciting people and perhaps you have become part of the local art system and have an exhibition here and there. So far, so good. Now, you have to ask yourself: Is this what you want? Is the city your goal? Are you a local artist now? Or is the city really a stepping stone to the international breakthrough you're hoping for? You quickly settle in somewhere and lose sight of the big picture. Progress can only ever happen when you move outside your comfort zone.

Affairs and brief liaisons. They bring relaxation and inspiration, but they are also very time-consuming. You should definitely live it up as much as you can and enjoy your younger years, but at some point it's time to take a break and prioritize your work. This doesn't exclude the possibility that you will be able to go back to where you left off later, when you are successful.

Alcohol and other drugs. Alcohol, the social drug par excellence, is, of course, widely used in the art world. Just because society accepts something doesn't mean it's good. With all addictive substances, everyone has to basically learn for themselves what they should better steer away from and where their limits are. Ruining your physical health is one thing, but alcohol and other drugs can inadvertently crush your mind and at times prevent you from doing your job.

Someone might claim for ten years that he or she can only do great things under the influence of lots of alcohol, and then, after ten years, realizes that he or she can work even better without it.

Accidents, illness, and overwork. Remember: You are your only employee. You mustn't take things easy, but you shouldn't overdo it either. Know your physical and mental limits, push yourself a bit further, because you're lazier than you think, but don't push yourself too far. Keep in mind the consequences.

Genius and madness. As some psychologists have already noted, the two are very close. Many artists have lost their mind on the road to success. Never lose touch with reality.

Fanaticism and misjudging yourself. You should be careful if you cross into the territory of opinionatedness and fanaticism. It is true that fanaticism can lead to incredible productivity, but it can also lead to an overestimation of your abilities and a misjudgment of yourself. Just because you work hard and are convinced of the quality of your work doesn't mean your output has substance and can hold its own in the art world.

Be open and curious

Not only is the world changing every day, but the art world and even its system are constantly changing, too. Sometimes fundamental things change abruptly and require quick action. Other changes come gradually, but are no less important. Be perceptive to change and keep up to date, so that you can respond dynamically to change. Do not obsessively close yourself off to progress. Look outside your box. The art world is part of a larger cosmos.

Broaden your horizons. Many artists believe the hub of the universe is wherever they happen to be. Those in North America think the world revolves around their city or maybe New York, while people in Europe or East Asia probably focus on themselves. Fortunately, everyone tends to be self-centered. However, the art world doesn't have a geographical center. Sure, the global art world has hotspots, and some are hugely more influential than others. But don't underestimate what's happening in the art world on other continents right now.

"Go and look at the other worlds. Make a friend or two there."

4.8. The free artist?

Society likes to see artists as people who are free. But how free are you as an artist, really? First, you want to become part of the artistic canon and be recognized in the art system. Second, you need to cover your basic needs, such as housing, food, and so on.

To gain recognition in the art system, you must follow the paths and rules of the art system, or at least make use of the system in the remotest sense. How consistently you do that is up to you, but it usually has a direct impact on how you are perceived in the art system, and accordingly, to your career and degree of recognition.

If you want to be able to cover your basic needs with your art at the same time, you must monetize your art. Consequently, as an artist, you have to make yourself dependent on other players in the system, too, and meet their expectations and needs. However, you will rarely get a guarantee from the outset that your commitment will eventually pay off.

Therefore, you should definitely not describe artists as being as free as society supposedly perceives them to be. Nevertheless, you have a lot of freedom within the system.

4.9. The positive power of art

"The mother of human evolution is creativity and art is its crowning achievement."

Did you get through the previous chapters? And you haven't put the book down yet? Then there's a little break now, before we move on to the demands of the art world. Despite this book's focus on professionalism, we must never forget: Art possesses a huge positive power. Art unites people with a common interest. It connects across generations, across continents, across cultures, even across languages. It is an expression of human creativity. Art can convey things that cannot be told in words or captured by other means. Art transcends even the boundaries of literature, music, dance, theater, and film. It can inspire people and stimulate new thoughts that go far beyond art, and thus bear new fruit.

"Art can give meaning to life."

As an artist, you're right in the middle of it. Art can be an expression of your deepest concerns and feelings. It can free you from your burdens. It can enable you to communicate.

Never forget why you make art. You do it because it fulfills you, because it takes you forward, because you enjoy it. Because it gives meaning to your life.

5. Your demeanor as an artist

To some extent, the art world is a stage. You appear there, and you are expected to play and fulfill a role. In today's world, the public sees artists and their artwork as inextricably linked. Take advantage of this. As an artist, you should be a memorable character. Alternatively, create an alter ego for when you appear in public. Last but not least, make sure you're generally socially acceptable.

5.1. Your artist persona

Who you are and how you are perceived is up to you. This applies equally to your outward appearance as well as what you say, and consequently, the image other people have of you. The outside world expects you to be an "artist," and so you can deliberately make use of stereotypical images of artists. However, don't exaggerate so much that you make a fool of yourself. Your interest in art and your occupation as an artist go a long way to creating an authentic demeanor, without you noticing it.

Basically, it's about three things: First, you should be recognizable as an artist. Second, you can be identified as a personality in your own right among your peers. And third, the story of you and your work should be coherent and interesting.

Let yourself be recognizable as an artist

Of course, there is no automatic way of distinguishing artists from non-artists. And yet there are people who you just know are artists. Some are more extroverted and a little extravagant. However, this doesn't suit everyone and under no circumstances should you adopt an image that you can't completely handle. This would appear more ridiculous than authentic, and, in the worst case, could even be annoying. Other artists are more introverted, often clothed in black from head to foot in order to attract as little attention as possible. And yet you still recognize them. There are many more types, but what they all have in common is that you can recognize them as artists if you want to. Take your pick. However, avoid being scruffy or unkempt.

Be identifiable as a personality in your own right

It's a fact that distinctiveness is a huge help in networking. For example, if your style is consistent, you make it easier for other people to remember you. But sometimes your foreign accent combined with the different, but always eye-catching earrings you always wear is enough. Or your extravagant sneakers, and so forth.

Now, let's talk about your name. It might seem quite obvious to some, but not to others. Most artists use their birth name, but this is not mandatory. Your name in the art world is up to you. You can modify your birth name or invent a completely new name. But you shouldn't be overly worried about your name, because in most cases it doesn't need changing. Basically, it should simply be unique and not too complicated. If your name is Frida Kahlo or Pablo Picasso, you should modify it or change it altogether, because it is already prominently in use. If your name is Manjula or Apu Nahasapeemapetilon, it is recommended to abbreviate your last name. Theoretically, a long or complicated name can also be your trademark, but this is rather the exception.

The story of you and your work

The statements about yourself, and also about your work, should be plausible and interesting. People want to hear stories. By omitting or emphasizing certain details about your life and art, you can give certain defined aspects of your demeanor a certain amount of color and create suspense without having to invent anything. As an artist, you meet a lot of people and usually only have short conversations with them. Individual statements are thus weighted more heavily. The people you talk to cannot usually place you as a person in a context, because they don't know you. This can quickly create false impressions and it is therefore advisable to develop and rehearse your story beforehand with the help of friends. It also helps if your story is individual and remarkable, so that everyone remembers you. Make yourself attractive – without appearing false or pushy.

You have to be able to hold your own in conversations. Questions about your art will soon be asked, too, such as what kind of art you produce, or what matters to you in your artistic practice. Here, you need to have the right answers ready.

You also have the option of creating an alter ego, an artist persona that is different than your real self. You can give it certain characteristics at will and wear it like a second skin in public.

Most of the time, however, as mentioned above, it's enough to focus on certain things and you're also allowed to embellish individual stories. In this context, we can argue about where artistic freedom begins and where it ends. For example, there are artists who alter their age or origin. Making rash, emotional, or ego-driven decisions is not recommended, but if you know something is actually preventing you from succeeding, then adjust what needs adjusting.

Joseph Beuys probably took it to the extreme in embellishing his vita with his famous crash in a dive bomber during the Second World War. The story was exaggerated, but had a true core in the legend of his life. By adding a rescue anecdote by alleged Crimean Tatars, who are said to have saved him from freezing to death by wrapping him in fat and felt, he created a quasi-mythical background through his near-death experience and at the same time a basis for the answer to the question of why he later created art precisely with these materials.

The artist who works in the shadows

There are artists who are insecure, shy, or extremely introverted. As a rule, it is recommended that you work on resolving such issues to the point where you can actively participate in the art world. Friends can help you in the beginning, and you can then learn to deal with it step by step.

However, these traits can also be intrinsic to an artist's personality – although it doesn't make your existence as an artist any easier. In this case, too, the personality must be well rehearsed and you must be able to answer questions. You also need to find a way to communicate with the outside world and how you can be perceived as an artist.

History has produced some examples that you can copy from.

5.2. Cultivate your brand

"Create a universe with you in the middle of it."

"Your brand is you and your art."

Your brand is the sum of your artist persona and your art. Your brand is rarely created overnight and only in a few cases can you draft a brand on the drawing board alone. The brand grows with you in a process that you consciously control. It can therefore adapt to your changing interests, but also to changes in the art world. Your brand needs to be visible and the ongoing process of cultivating it is responsible for that.

What is meant by cultivating a brand in the context of art? First, it's producing and publishing your art. Second, it's cultivating your demeanor as an artist. And third, it's cultivating your social circles in the art world. This way, your brand is transported to the outside world and can firmly establish itself in the art world.

Cultivate your image as an exciting artistic personality. Share your life with other people, whether it's through newsletters, invitations to your birthday party, or social networks such as Instagram etc. Learn to be a good host. Being exciting and able to arouse people's curiosity can open doors for you.

Your brand sets you apart from other artists. It's not just your art, it's also the parts of your artist persona – that is, your reputation, your history, your previous career – that make up your brand. That's why it's so important to nurture your brand. People don't just want your work, they want the story and the image to go with it!

5.3. General social acceptability

Besides your role as an artist, where you don't always have to conform to all the conventions of society, you are still a social being who interacts with other people. You must understand that there are patterns of behavior that can make you likeable and pave the way to your success. And charismatic people have a clear advantage. Strong characters assert themselves better. You win people over with genuine sympathy.

Be friendly without losing your focus

People want to be treated with respect. Good manners don't hurt. Be friendly, of course not excessively so, otherwise you risk that people will no longer take you seriously and, if you try to be Mother Teresa, you'll never get any work done.

Find a good mix of friendliness, helpfulness, and determination.

Be communicative and sociable

Communication and conviviality are the foundations of networking. And they create important friendships. Making it in the art world all by yourself is practically impossible. If you find these skills difficult, join someone who is communicative or sociable, and participate in the art world with them. However, you shouldn't spend all your time socializing, because your work comes first.

The exhausting artist

Some people describe working or collaborating with artists as exhausting. Do you think that applies to you? Why is collaboration exhausting and does it have to be that way, or is there something you can do as an artist to stop being so exhausting? What does that mean for you? Or are the people you work with not sufficiently tolerant and able to take pressure? Or do you or your counterpart perhaps lack experience in some way? At the end of the day, the effort of all those involved must be in proportion to the return they receive. Otherwise, there is a risk that collaboration will end abruptly or that people will talk about you behind your back.

5.4. Interaction with other artists

In the course of your artistic career, you will encounter countless other artists and it makes a lot of sense to have constructive interactions with fellow artists from the beginning.
It's okay to make yourself the center of attention, but still be respectful in your interactions with your colleagues. There are always artists who

are looking for confrontation. Defend yourself, but don't waste unnecessary energy on such arguments.

Sometimes, people talk about other artists behind their backs. Withdraw from such conversations, as soon as they start getting personal.

There are many artists who only talk about themselves and their art and are not interested in your art. Dialog always involves listening to each other.

Artist friendships

Artist friendships are incredibly rewarding and very valuable at every stage of your career and in different endeavors. A fine example is Matisse and Picasso, who, despite their different conceptions of art, inspired each other enormously. Create opportunities for such friendships to develop.

Helpful fellow artists are those who can most easily answer your questions. Some are further up the career ladder than you, others are at your level. You will certainly be asked for advice at some point, too. Smart artists realize that it's more fun to move up the ladder together – and it's often easier, too.

Friendships with fellow artists can be the most valuable friendships for you. You are all in the same boat and you already have a lot in common.

"Be loyal to your artist friends."

Rivalry and envy

In fact, there is much less rivalry in art today than is often perceived. To become successful – as this book attempts to explain – many factors must be right, and your actual works of art are only one of them. For example, an artist can be quick to think that he or she can keep up with a colleague. In reality, though, he or she lacks important qualities to be able to win the metaphorical race – but he or she is not necessarily aware of this. Let's assume that the art of the two artists in our example is roughly of equal value. In this case, the race will still be won by the artist who has the right interpretation at hand; whose age, origin, and gender fit; and who has the right experience in his or her résumé. You think you can compete, but actually you're seriously overestimating yourself.

Nevertheless, with a healthy dose of self-confidence and enough self-reflection, competition can spur you on to great achievement.

"Envy sucks."

Envy makes no sense. As mentioned, it's often unwarranted, because you actually don't stand a chance. So, if you're both a good and hard-working artist, and if you work specifically on your success, you'll get there eventually. Just try to be better than the person you envy and understand what advantage this person seems to have.

And avoid speaking ill of someone or their work out of envy or wanting to harm them. It doesn't make you or your work any better and it's simply unprofessional, embarrassing, and most of all very unsportsmanlike.

The me-first people

Putting yourself out there is part of business, but me-first people are just annoying. They spread an unconstructive and sometimes hyper-competitive mood and thus harm not only themselves but also those around them. In the art world, you don't make it to the top alone. You need friends and a team. Me-first people lack this mindset and so, sooner or later, shut the door on themselves.

Mutual inspiration

Do not claim to be the sole author and owner of a technique, formal language, or theme. Other artists in the world had and have the same thoughts. And last but not least: Thanks to the Internet and social media, ideas and thoughts now spread around the globe at the speed of light, often unconsciously.

"If you think you have a revolutionary idea, keep it to yourself until you're ready to share it with the whole world."

Just as you are inspired by other artists, you will inspire other artists. The more time artists spend together, the more likely it is that their techniques and themes will overlap unnoticed. This will happen with the fellow artists around you first. If you think you can see traits of your work in other people's work, do not overestimate yourself, and avoid pointless and misguided conflicts, especially with colleagues. Learn to deal with it confidently.

If you take, you must also give. If you can inspire other artists, regard it as praise for your own work.

6. Your art

"It doesn't matter what you do. It's just important that you do it."

Maybe it was easier to be an artist in the last century. The young generation of artists at the time was happy to throw everything old overboard or break down boundaries, creating something new and unprecedented. In fact, many forms and techniques were tried out without a binding formal language prevailing. That is, formally speaking, the whole field was probably staked out. The expansion of the field, from a purely formal perspective, today usually happens across genres (music, theater, dance, literature, and so on) or is rooted in technological progress.

"With one foot in tradition and one foot in the avant-garde (future)."

Of course, in terms of form, there are still niches and nuances that an artist can carve out as independent and authentic art, but new art increasingly distinguishes itself from previous art through its content. Here, there is still plenty of space on the field. Through social changes, new land is always added that can be tilled.

"To make true art, you need to have a serious calling. A need to work on it. A need to work through something. A calling is supernatural. If you have a real calling it will be heard."

The focus is shifting more and more to artists. While at the beginning of the last century, the work was still the main focus, there are more and more artists who showcase themselves and thus become part of their work. This trend can also be observed in society, and culminates in social media.

6.1. Develop an understanding of art

General knowledge of art

Before you can even make art, you must first develop an understanding of art and the artistic canon. Develop a general knowledge of art.

Your focus should be on contemporary art, because this is where you will find the artists who are relevant today and to whom you will be compared. However, you still need to know what happened in art history.

You must know names such as Raphael, Michelangelo, Leonardo da Vinci, Albrecht Dürer, Peter Paul Rubens, Titian, Katsushika Hokusai, Rembrandt van Rijn, and so on.

But more important for you is what happened from about 1900. This is where you need to be knowledgeable, and you should also have in-depth knowledge of specialized areas that affect your work.

Never forget: The view of past art is always a subjective one. Perhaps there are artists and theories of art to which little attention is paid in your environment, but which are no less relevant to the artistic canon. And the future will certainly look more global, multiethnic, and feminine than the artistic canon has been until now.

Philosophy and theory

Some artists specifically refer to philosophical-theoretical texts in their work. It is not mandatory for every artist to study philosophy and theory, but it can be enlightening and enriching. For certain art movements or deeper insights into the work of some artists, selected texts are helpful or even necessary. Possible names include: Arthur C. Danto, Gilles Deleuze, Michel Foucault, Judith Butler, Jean-Paul Sartre, Félix Guattari, and Walter Benjamin etc.

Stay up to date

The global art world comprises a sea of information, with new artists and new knowledge being added all the time. Use media such as magazines, books, and the Internet, in order to keep up.

You need to visit exhibitions regularly, but museum tours, talks, and symposia are also important opportunities to feel the pulse of the art world. You can visit good and relevant exhibitions and events mainly in big cities. It therefore makes a lot of sense to live in such a city, too. As well as visiting exhibitions, you can cultivate your network. Do this by going to the openings of exhibitions.

Nationally: Find out which galleries and institutions within your reach are important. Have a list of exhibition locations and galleries whose programs you follow, regularly consult the art events calendar for your region.
You don't have to go to every exhibition. It is actually very difficult to find the right balance between regular exhibition visits, networking, and concentration on the work in the studio.
It is advisable to visit between one and three exhibitions every two weeks.

Nationally and internationally: Are there art fairs and biennales near you? Make a list of the most important art events. Usually, there are several dates a year when different galleries and exhibition locations stage exhibitions together. These have names such as season opening, art walk, art week, gallery weekend, first Thursdays, and so on. All these larger events also attract audiences from more distant regions and abroad. Be aware of this higher visibility. Familiarize yourself with the scene. If you want to be part of it, it's helpful to be familiar with it.

Internationally: What art fairs and major art events (biennales, and so on) can you get to within half a day?
A recommendation for artists in Europe (in addition to regular exhibition attendance): documenta in Kassel every five years, the Biennales in Venice every two years, one or two art fairs from the top five every year: Art Basel (Basel, Miami, Hong Kong), The Armory Show (New York), FIAC (Paris), Art Cologne (Cologne), and Frieze (London, New York, Los Angeles).

Visit major cities around the world on a regular basis and check out the art scenes there.

Talk about art

You're not just supposed to consume or produce art, you're also supposed to process it mentally. Talk regularly about the exhibitions you have visited, about your art, about art in general, with your fellow students, friends, and so on. You can learn a lot about art this way. If this isn't possible in your life, then you must make it possible. Visit other artists, talk to them at art openings, organize informal meetings in your studio or a bar.

6.2. Your studio

A studio is essential for any artist. The studio is not only a working space, but also a thinking space. It gives you the opportunity to shut out everyday life in order to concentrate fully on your art. It should be a place for creativity. While there are some artists today who work without a studio, the positive and dynamic force inherent in a studio should not be underestimated or forgotten.

Every artist has different ideas and needs for their ideal studio, and often you can't afford the perfect studio right from day one. Usually, demands also grow over time.

Shared studios – where several artists share space for their work – are widespread. They have many advantages, such as sharing costs and tools, exchanging ideas and information, and motivating each other. However, they also harbor potential for conflict and distraction.

Your studio should be set up in such a way that it prevents obstacles getting in the way of your creative work and facilitates smooth working processes. Working undisturbed also means not being distracted by having to look for the right pencil, brush, or tool. Order is therefore not an end in itself, but helps you to work without interruption. In fact, it's crucial to have in your studio all the tools and materials you need to work without a break.

"Your studio should be your perfect art production facility."

However, a studio is not only a space for working and thinking, but offers even more. It's also a warehouse and a showroom and generally makes you appear professional as an artist. It gives you the opportunity to invite fellow artists and discuss your work with them. Here, you can showcase yourself and your works, and receive potential business partners and customers (gallery owners, collectors, and so on). Immerse them in your world and allow them to see and experience your works.

Always keep in mind that your studio can also significantly influence your perception – and therefore your art. For example, in a small, low-ceilinged studio, you will automatically produce primarily small works, whereas larger works tend to be created in a large studio.

6.3. Your work process

Artists struggle all the time to find the optimal state for working. It's not easy. Let's call it the quadrilateral problem, comprising time, money, inspiration, and motivation. All four things are necessary in the right proportion to be able to work productively. You need time to go to the studio; you need money to afford materials, studio time, or external labor; you need inspiration, in other words, an idea; and you must be motivated, so that the process of production can start. Below are a few suggestions about this, although the problems of time and money will not be discussed further here, because they are too individual.

However, it's not only about producing something or anything, but also about reflecting on it and verifying it later. You have to ascertain whether what you produce meets your requirements and those of art.

Inspiration

"To be able to create art, you also have to think about art. Only if you drink art, can you also piss (produce) art."

For inspiration as well as for motivation, many artists find it enormously beneficial to be exposed to a constant stream of art on a daily basis, be it via the Internet, books, at art school, or at exhibitions. Please note, however: For the actual production of art, many artists withdraw completely and avoid outside influences of any kind, in order to exclude distractions.

Art itself offers you a huge pool to draw inspiration from. Other genres, such as music, film, literature, and so on, can also serve you well. And, not least, life offers you many sources of inspiration.

"Use your art as an outlet. It can serve to offload any emotionality, both positive and negative."

Find out what inspires and stimulates you. Observe and analyze yourself and use your insight to then go to those exact places or perform those actions that fire your spirit if you're ever struggling for inspiration.

Maybe nature can give you what you need? Travel always offers new impressions. Here, reference should be made to the study abroad and funded residencies. They are not only good for your résumé, for networking or as a break, but also as a reliable source of new inspiration.

Talk to fellow artists, because quite often dialog with other artists helps you to find new thoughts and to define existing ones more precisely. Even people who don't come from the art world can sometimes give you completely different perspectives that will help you move forward. Perhaps you just need a friend, a partner, or a muse to inspire you to work. But don't get distracted!

Motivation

Inspiration alone is not enough, you also need to find the motivation to realize your ideas. Many artists have countless ideas and yet their storage space or portfolio is yawningly empty. People – whether they are gallery owners or curators – want to see something tangible, at least in the beginning, when you haven't yet established a reputation for yourself.

Create an environment that puts you in a productive and, at best, positive work mood, one that consciously or subconsciously motivates you. A shared studio made up of hardworking artists, for example, can motivate you to be hardworking, too.

Dyed-in-the-wool artists inherently have the urge to produce art, but even they sometimes struggle with motivation. The same applies here as for inspiration: Use your experience to motivate yourself.

Draw on your emotionality and use it to drive you. Can you work better when you are agitated or when you are calm? Analyze yourself and take advantage of these productive moments in your studio. You can also learn to induce a state of being agitated – including avoiding possible collateral damage and side effects. Or do you need an antithesis, something to ground you, so you can reach your optimal working state?

Having goals increases your motivation. Exhibition dates and the like can motivate you to work hard. Make sure other people set goals for you, such as through an exhibition invitation – or set your own goals. Set your goals so that the pressure is appropriate for you. Some artists need a lot of pressure, while others are paralyzed by it.

Reflection

"Reflection separates the wheat from the chaff, regarding both art and the artist."

Just because you consider yourself an artist doesn't mean you actually make art. Constantly questioning your work anew and positioning it in the artistic canon is one of the most important processes that you as an artist must always initiate.

Only by critically examining your works in the artistic canon will you know if you have succeeded in generating actual added value in art. And this critical examination gives you indications of how to formulate and convey your message even more precisely.

Talk to lots of people about your work. Learn to listen. What do other people see in your work? Is what they see the same as what you want them to see? What other artists are you compared to?

6.4. Aspects of your art

If you engage with the artistic canon (which is essential), and are thus inspired by other artists, then you automatically acquire techniques, visual languages, or themes. This is a natural process, it often happens without you being aware of it, and it is part of becoming an artist. But acquiring these things alone is not enough, you must also understand them. Your art requires conscious decisions, you need to be aware of the aspects and their meaning in your art. Form, material, execution, content, and so on all require conscious decisions.

"To make true art, it takes more than a little remixing of what exists."

Theoretically, there are almost no limits to art. Nevertheless, it can reach its limits the moment it deviates too far from the canon and is no longer accepted as art. It must then either move closer to the canon or the canon must be worked on until it includes it.

Try yourself out at the beginning of your artistic career; use this as a process to be able to find yourself. Experiment. Break the habits in the way you work. Train yourself to deal with the things that are less familiar to you. If you like to paint fast, try painting slowly. If you paint small pictures, try painting big pictures. If you build installations out of dozens of different materials, try to limit yourself to three, and so on. Even if you have considerable experience: Always look for a challenge. This will stop you repeating yourself and becoming monotonous.

Form and technique

There are artists who claim that the form and technique of works are determined by the content. This should not be seen as absolute, but it is a reasonable starting point, because some forms and techniques are clearly better suited to certain content. Also, each material has its connotation and not every statement can be conveyed in a suitable way with every material. Always question whether you have chosen the right means for your statement.

Of course, you need to master the technique of producing your work, but don't get lost in perfecting it. Sooner than you think, you'll lose sight of the big picture.

"Learn when it's time to stop working on a piece. It's not uncommon for a painting to be painted to death, because an artist carried on for too long."

In principle, there is nothing against you working across genres and styles – seen over the entire span of your creative work – but it's important that observers can recognize how this came about or can see that it is somehow connected.

Be aware that the different forms of artistic expression also have different advantages and disadvantages, not only in and of themselves, but also in terms of your career. Installations, but also large sculptures, for example, are practically unmarketable in the early stages of a career. On the other hand, they generate a different kind of attention compared with painting, for example.

Galleries are usually interested mainly in art for which a buyer base exists, primarily flat art works such as paintings and art that is manageable in terms of its size. Bulky and hard-to-sell items are not infrequently just "showpieces" or "decoration," or, simply put, marketing for galleries, whereas for institutions such as museums, sales are not the first priority and elaborate installations can also be supported with production budgets. Here, we shouldn't forget funding programs, residencies, and so on, which again may have different preferences and conditions. Considerations about this are not meant to push you into a particular medium, but such thoughts will help you develop an understanding of how things are connected.

Content and statement

In principle, the content of art can be everything. You can address consumer society, social injustices, natural phenomena, or simply your fucked-up life in your work. You determine the content of your art. But not all content meets with the same level of interest from the public and art experts.

"Art has the ability to make important and serious issues accessible, without the observer having to be in the middle of it."

Whether you want to say something with the work is up to you. In any case, your work needs a backstory. People want to hear stories and they want to understand why you're creating this art. This not only concerns visitors to your exhibition, but also collectors, gallery owners, or curators. Your art needs content when it is still in your studio. If you don't have any content for it, then you have to invent some. In some cases, the content does not emanate from the works, but rather from the artist's exceptional persona, which itself gives the works meaning and content.

"Art is a subconscious and conscious treatment and materialization of thoughts."

Things can quickly look like art, but they should also be understood. Your art must be translated into language, so that it can be accessible to people. Language is, so to speak, the only generally understandable means of communication and must make your art tangible.

There are actually people who create good art, but can't explain it themselves because they work intuitively, for example. The lack of such an explanation of art is a problem today. If this applies to you, you need to charge someone with interpreting and contextualizing what you have created. The resulting story is the one you tell in the future.

First and foremost, it's not about retaining the interpretive sovereignty over your art, but giving people a point of reference. How your art is ultimately perceived is another matter. If, in the end, the reception of your art is completely different than the one you intended, it is up to you to accept this or to specifically take countermeasures.

With all the artistic freedom you have in establishing the stories about your works, you should still not take it to extremes. You don't need to invent complex worlds. In the best case, the story about your works or cycles of works should be short and insightful. Don't interpret anything into your work that doesn't suit you or make sense. Always remain as authentic as possible and don't claim things that you can't sustain over a long period of time.

Self-perceived or society-imposed weaknesses or disadvantages in your life do not necessarily have to be hidden or suppressed. They can also become part of your story or content of your work.

Social and political themes are readily seized on in art. One can now ask how personal the engagement with such themes really is, or whether the topic is simply used to generate attention. Both are absolutely legitimate and "part of the game."

Periodically, there are very one-sided, blatant artworks and opinions about controversial topics. This may be permissible in the context of art. Nevertheless, artists should always be aware that their statements are one-sided and the truth is often more complex.

"Art is interested in politics, but politics isn't usually interested in art."

If your art contains text or language that isn't English, please always provide a translation. Your art should be given the opportunity to be understood. If you rule that out from the start, it's a shame and at times unprofessional.

"Your audience is the world. It should understand your work."

Draw from your life, from your surroundings, from your time.

Titling

The titles of works have gained enormously in importance over the last hundred years. With conceptual art at the latest, they became an integral part of the creation of works. Titles can be so central today that they give meaning to the work in the first place.

The titles can be part of the work. They can be part of the statement or content. They can be part of your style. Always think carefully about titles. Should they be precise? Or rather vague and open to interpretation? The final decision will be yours, but perhaps someone can help you find a suitable title. It makes sense if the titles in one creative period arise from the same world of thought. A catchy title is more likely to stick with observers, but may also miss the opportunity to give the work depth.

You might also decide against giving your work a specific title. Then you always have the option of using "Untitled." That's also a title. If you

wish, you can record a working title that is descriptive by using paren-
theses. For example, if you have a sculpture of a donkey with a cat, you
can call it "Untitled (Donkey with Cat)." If you have a series of works,
the works can also be numbered consecutively, for example, "Untitled
I" and so on.

In short: Always give your works a title. Even "Untitled" is a title.

Reception

Reception refers to how your art is perceived and interpreted by others,
both within and outside the art system. You cannot fully influence how
your art is received by individuals. But, by preparing the content of your
work so that it can be easily absorbed and understood by the observer,
and by speaking as clear a language as possible in your work, you can
convey a clear message.

An additional formulated text on the content of the work can also be
helpful. You can either write this text yourself or hire someone to do it
for you. In the "professional" exhibition business, additional texts and
information on works, artists, and the exhibition are standard and are
usually written by the curators or other staff members. Normally, your
work is placed in the big picture and in terms of art history. Sometimes
you recognize things in your own work that you were not aware of before.

If you release your art into the art world largely without comment, it
will be received and interpreted by others. In the worst case, this can
sometimes bring about reputation-damaging misinterpretations and it
remains misunderstood or is deprived of its status as art.

*"Many artists are heavily preoccupied with themselves and their work, so
it's easy for others to instrumentalize their work."*

Keep in mind that sometimes the appreciation of your art comes from
a completely different motivation than yours. And the more successful
you become with your work, the more this dynamic is reinforced. People then become correspondingly less concerned with your works in

themselves. Either the representative and financial value of your work is in the foreground for them, or its content – which is often bent into shape by curators and other theorists – takes center stage.

The pulse of time

The world is always changing and so is art and its content, themes, and concerns. There are always trends and fashions, whether you want to follow them, submit to them, ignore them, or intentionally go against them is up to you, but you should at least know about them.

Being at the forefront of trends as an artist can give you a lot of confidence and also generate attention. Whether the trend endures and ultimately finds its way into art history is another question.

What is "out" can also be "in" again later. For example, there were times when only a few people were interested in painting. Today, it's more popular than ever.

Technical developments are also progressing steadily. Perhaps technical advances can add to your art, simplify its production, or make it completely obsolete. If you're a sculptor, for example, the advent of affordable large 3D printers can significantly impact your work.

Artistic freedom

"Not all art has to be critical, but it has the freedom to be."

Art is allowed to explore the boundaries of morality, law, and religion. Accordingly, artists can usually enjoy the freedom to act as a contemporary critical witness to humanity without having to fear any consequences. But where the boundaries of artistic freedom ultimately lie is strongly defined by the society in which the art happens, and is thus also subject to change.

This freedom is one of the most important foundations of art and must be both won and defended, but it must also know its own limits in order to continue to exist.

A piece of advice if you use, for example, photographic and video material from external sources in your own works: Some artists worry about copyright infringement and written warnings. As a rule, the use of material without the consent of its author is not permitted, but if the material is accessible through legal channels and the work ultimately becomes valuable in terms of art and is also published exclusively in the context of art, you will very rarely be prosecuted as a visual artist.

6.5. Dealing with criticism and its influence

"Don't take criticism to heart, but instead add it to your mind."

Criticism is a part of how you reflect on your work. It is an assessment of your art that can be very helpful. Therefore, you should always take it seriously, but also assess it and place it in context to determine its truthfulness and relevance. The following questions will help you: How professional is the criticism? How relevant and accomplished is the critic in the art system? How objective is the criticism? What is its motivation? In what frame of mind or mood is the critic? How close are you to the critic?

This is about both positive and negative criticism. And, of course, you have to distinguish between criticism that happens in public, criticism that happens in a protected environment, and purely private criticism between two people.

Once you have analyzed everything, you ultimately have to ask yourself: What can I take out of this for my art and myself? Or was it simply well-intentioned praise that is actually irrelevant? Or a jealous colleague who doesn't like the look of me?

If you receive public criticism, good or bad, consider it a gift, because it means you are being noticed. Besides, negative criticism can hurt you much less today than it did a hundred years ago.

Many artists who are successful today were misunderstood at the beginning. Conversely, being misunderstood is by no means the key to success. On the contrary, the path to understanding must be paved by you.

6.6. Development

You will develop and you must develop. This applies not only to your art, but also to the circumstances of your work.

Once you have defined yourself and your art, you still go through different creative phases in your artistic life. The works from each phase will differ, this is called development and it is very important. Otherwise, you're repeating yourself and just treading water. No one can say how far these creative phases will ultimately depart from your beginnings or how your definition will change.

Several works with a similar formal language or a similar concern can be combined into cycles of works. Use cycles of works as a tool. Always try to create several works in the same style before switching to another. This makes your art less arbitrary, despite changes in style, and can, for example, create incentives for collectors to want to own works from different creative phases, or prompt galleries and museums to want to present new creative phases.

If you get increased attention from the art world, it's important to optimize your output to the point where you can keep up with the opportunities you are given, both in the marketplace and in exhibition circles. But always keep in mind the interests that are basically driving the individual players. Don't let yourself be instrumentalized into something that you yourself can't sustain in the long run and that doesn't benefit you – unless it gets you the golden parachute in the process and you are also willing to take that route.

As mentioned earlier, you need to be able to keep up with the demands of the art world's players. If you want to establish yourself in the art market, it is usually beneficial to produce a lot. It's like a cake: The bigger it is, the more guests you can invite. The art market today is huge, so you should have enough goods at the ready. Picasso allegedly created tens of thousands of works during his lifetime. This is certainly one of the reasons why he is still omnipresent today. However, this does not mean that you should flood the market with paintings that might be poor quality. That will backfire. Nevertheless: Being a successful artist is not for lazy people, you must always work hard and set yourself high standards.

"The more you have created, the harder it is to erase you."

The more successful you become, the more experienced and active your business partners usually become. More (and more specialized) personnel become available. For example, complex projects or demanding artists will quickly become too much of a challenge for a small gallery, but are easier for larger galleries to handle. In return, the expectations placed on you will probably become greater, as well.

Optimize your studio operations

For some artists it may be natural to hand over certain tasks, but for others it is not. At the latest when you are successful, you will have to learn to delegate certain things – even if it's just your accounts. But even for young artists who are starting out, handing over certain things or steps can work wonders. Basically, you don't need to produce your art yourself. This is not a new idea – Rembrandt also ran a workshop where employees and students painted on behalf of and for him. However, it makes a lot of sense to know your craft well anyway, if only to be able to give competent and correct instructions or to create templates and prototypes.

There are things that take up a disproportionate amount of your time and/or nerves. It can be devastating when simple tasks destroy your motivation and thus hinder your production. For example, if you have a problem assembling and priming your canvases, put it off for days, and your production is at a standstill, then it's better to work in a café for two hours and give a fellow student 30 dollars to do it for you in an afternoon.

"Your motivation must never suffer, your task is art."

Use the competencies of external partners and specialists. Experts can produce custom and special designs for you that would take a lot of time and effort for you to make – or maybe you wouldn't be able to make them at all. And, not least, the quality of the work performed by specialists can be much higher.

Work optimization starts, for example, with having an assistant who can lend you a helping hand. If you can't afford assistants yet, but still have the promise of a large budget for a piece of art, you can also use art production companies. These are companies that specialize in the realization of anything from individual works of art to entire exhibitions.

Giving over the production of works of art or steps in the production process opens up new opportunities. It expands your creative scope enormously. You can work on more complex and/or larger projects and, of course, produce more.

Think of your studio not just as a place to work, but at some point as the home of a small business that, with one or two employees or maybe more, will advance your art career.

Costs: realization versus budget

You shouldn't save money on art. On the contrary, you need to invest in yourself and your art. Only those who invest can win. However, this is not to say that you should now spend your money pointlessly on artists' materials. Some artists these days tend to buy everything from often overpriced specialty art supply stores. But for many things, there are cheaper and sometimes better alternatives in hardware or general retail stores.

Work within your budget. If you're short on cash, there's no point in going down a Jeff Koons path with mirror-polished stainless steel. Many things can be realized with less money. The first and supposedly perfect path is not always the right one. The beauty of your profession is: You are an artist, you set your own standards and you can decide for yourself what you want to realize and how – not to mention the fact that the original idea, which would cost many times more, is known by nobody but you. Little money can stimulate creativity. Often recycled or cheaper materials are quite sufficient.

"Start small. Get bigger. Save up money."

If, despite everything, you want an ultra-polished aesthetic, which is accordingly expensive, then your only options are to save money or raise funds.

If you want to realize projects that are beyond your financial means, you always have the option of looking for financiers such as galleries, collectors, museums, foundations, funding programs, and so on. Here, it is important to describe your project as precisely as possible. As well as sketches and models, you might want to use digital 3D visualizations, which can be very convincing today.

Another smart strategy is to approach projects in a similar way to Christo and Jeanne-Claude. They sold very high quality sketches of each of their planned projects until they had enough money to realize the project itself.

The thread that runs through your oeuvre

"Clarify your work! Make clear what your work is about."

There should always be a common thread running through your oeuvre (body of work), that is, all the works you produce throughout your artistic career. A high recognition factor can have a significant impact on a successful career as an artist. Keep in mind: What many successful artists have in common is that they have an unmistakable signature. Their works have a high recognition factor. They have developed their own style, which can be both visually and conceptually based. Develop your own aesthetic, your own concept, your own language in art.

"You have to feel it's right; that's important!"

In the beginning, it can be difficult for some artists to find their own individual style. Keep looking at your works and comparing them side by side, and try to see connections.

Get some orientation. A simple strategy to find yourself is to look around and see what is near you. Then, determine what separates you from that. Which artists work in a similar way? Which major or minor trends influence you? Try to place your work in the context of the artistic canon – with a focus on contemporary art.

6.7. Document and keep an inventory

Documenting is the second most important thing next to working! Document everything you do. And sort it!

Performances are fleeting. Installations usually have to be dismantled at some point; paintings are frequently in danger of being painted over or disappearing into some attic. Documentation is therefore often the only means by which works can be preserved and made available at any time. They must be available because you need them in order to reflect. This allows you to view all your works side by side, compare them with each other, and recognize developments.

Furthermore, you need regular documentation to be able to compile a portfolio – for example for an art award application. But besides jurors, also curators, gallery owners, and collectors should be able to get an overview of your work when you are in touch with them. Therefore, an always available portfolio (with a selection of the best and most recent works) is crucial for your career.

How should you document?

Initially, a good smartphone is enough these days. Document your work with photos. Document your performances with videos. If you don't have a filing system yet, the following is recommended: Always copy all material to your computer. Create a folder with the name "Art." Everything concerning your art goes in there – art school applications, art prize entries, research, cost estimates, project sketches, and so on. The works should be sorted by date. For each work or group of works, make a folder and name it with the date and title of the work. In such a way, you automatically always have order. All other documents you either file in the folders with the works or create new folders called, for example, "sketches" or "applications."

Write a short text for each work, noting its title and what the work is about. If you do this in your sketchbook, take a picture of it or scan it and put it on your computer in the folder for that particular piece. So you still know later what you were thinking when you did the work. You can also use voice recording or video sequences to capture your thoughts. It is important that you assign them to the individual works, so that everything is always together.

And remember: Back up your files regularly! Scan your sketchbooks regularly, too.

Inventory

Everything you declare as a work should be documented and entered in an inventory that includes all your works. The inventory is only for you personally. Galleries will ask for one sooner or later, but it is advisable not to let anyone know the exact extent of your inventory. In particular, the art market should not always know how many and what kind of works you have already produced: You can use this lack of knowledge to your advantage in different ways. If you are rich and famous at some point, you can disclose your inventory and publish it in a "catalogue raisonné."

So, keep an inventory. A simple text or Excel file with a folder for the photos is quite sufficient for the first few years. Later, when you have money and staff, you can use database software to manage your works.

In a list, sorted by date, all your works are itemized with: title, year, technique, size, price, and so on.

Always make a note of the date associated with a price, because prices change over time. It's important to know the price of a work before someone asks you. If you sell the work, note the name of the buyer, the name of the seller, the final price (including or excluding sales tax), and the date of sale. It is important that you know where your works are and who owns which work, so that they can be loaned out for exhibitions, for example, and so that you have an idea of where the works come from once they reach the secondary art market.

Portfolio

An up-to-date and digital portfolio is essential for every artist. If possible, create it with a layout program, such as Adobe InDesign, but if need be, you can also use Word. The final version of your portfolio must be a PDF file that you can then either print or send/upload digitally, as required.

Your portfolio should be well structured, neat, and clearly understandable. Especially with applications, it gives a first – and often last and lasting – impression of you. Carelessly created portfolios are sometimes immediately discarded by jurors. Make sure your portfolio is up to date and keep it as compact as possible. The best works should be at the beginning, because the first pages must be convincing. Often, only the very good portfolios are really looked at from beginning to end.

Your portfolio comprises: a cover page with your name and contact information, then a résumé section with your biography, art education, exhibition list, art awards/scholarships/residencies, bibliography including articles and reviews, and so on. The main section includes selected works with representative photos; one work per page as a guide. Each work must be labeled with title, year, material, and dimensions. If necessary, you can add a short text with background information for a better understanding. This should be as short and clear as possible. The works should be sorted chronologically in descending order, that is, the most recent should be listed first.

6.8. Artist collectives, artist groups, and collaborations

Unfortunately, as art history shows, artist collectives (duos and more) are rarely successful and rarely last. Some prominent exceptions prove the rule. Artists are distinct individualists and, sooner or later, most artist collectives break up. It is true that artist collectives are less agile and flexible and also have more trouble establishing themselves on the art market. Nevertheless, this kind of cooperation can be very fruitful and set the cornerstone for further individual work. Examples of collectives include Marina Abramović and Ulay, General Idea, Ruangrupa, Gilbert & George, and Fischli/Weiss.

In recent times, collaborations have become more common than collectives. A collaboration is less binding for the artist than working in a collective, and it is often initially limited to a selected project. However, if a collaboration with one or more partners is successful, this often leads to follow-up projects. The choice of partners for these collaborations is no longer limited to other artists – you have many different options: Collaborations in the areas of fashion, music, dance, literature, and so on are common practice today, as are collaborations in the form of all other conceivable commercial and non-commercial projects.

Artist groups, in other words, artists who devoted themselves to a common cause to a greater or less extent, were often formative and influential for art history, but unfortunately hardly exist in the present. Looking ahead, it would be desirable to have more artist groups again. Examples of groups include Guerrilla Girls, ZERO, Die Brücke (The Bridge), and CoBrA.

7. The ten commandments

What you must do, without fail.

7.1. Everything for art

"You are a slave to your art."

If you want to become a successful artist, then you have to put art before your personal needs. Art always comes first – in every case and practically without exception. This is important to internalize and strictly adhere to. You must submit to the rules of art.

You must be boringly studious. You need tremendous self-discipline. Put private matters aside. All your energy must be devoted to your art. If you spend less than 50% of your energy on art, then stop doing art. The approach to adopt is: Move almost exclusively in artistic circles.

Your self must adapt to the needs of your art. If your art requires you to be a vegetarian, then you will be a vegetarian from tomorrow.
What do you do if you're at an opening and a disagreeable but successful and relevant artist asks you to join him later for drinks with selected guests? You go – regardless of whether you're on the guest list of your favorite party (where you had actually planned to go) or your young lover wants to go home with you. With every decision in your life, you must always ask yourself: Which decision is better for my art and my art career?

"You have to breathe art, eat art, rub it on yourself, etc."

You must always be ready as an artist to do what is necessary to further your career. It doesn't matter if you feel like it, if it's Sunday, if it's early in the morning, if it's late at night.

7.2. Learn from established artists

"Learn from the masters."

Study what preoccupied the old masters, but most importantly, what preoccupies today's established artists and how they have behaved at various stages of their artistic careers. Use them as a guide and inspiration. They mastered many of the problems and questions that bother you – whether it's the content of their work, their interaction with the art system, overcoming a career crisis, or setting up a large studio business with staff.

7.3. Work! Work!

"Nothing comes from nothing!"

"A rule for the beginning of your career: In order for you to sell one work, you must produce 15."

No matter how great your will and vision are, gallery owners, collectors, curators, and so on all want to see action and facts. That's what matters in the end – not your ramblings.

Work a lot, work hard. Practice makes perfect. Your artistic development is largely driven by your ongoing work.

Stay focused on your artistic work. It's okay to curate an exhibition space on the side, but never forget, you are an artist, not a curator. The focus must be on your art.

Allow yourself rest periods in between. They are important and they can also give you new inspiration, but they should always be deliberately planned with a beginning and an end. Otherwise, you run the risk of slipping into a state of inertia.

There is no excuse for not working. If you're not working, then you're not really pursuing the goal of becoming a successful artist. Basta!

Overcome your weaker self. Your weaker self will always tell you that the work you have done is sufficient, but don't be deceived. Good art requires stepping out of your comfort zone. Otherwise, you will produce mediocrity at best and that will never be enough to become successful.

"Good art causes problems. Good art tugs at your nerves. Good art is too big, too complex for your small studio. Good art is beyond the scope of your budget. Good art requires an extra trip to the art supply store or hardware store. Good art needs something after closing time. Good art requires overtime. Good art doesn't just fit in the trunk of your car. Good art can't just be sent by regular mail. Good art is exhausting."

7.4. Think big!

"Set yourself ambitious goals!"

Basically, it's already an incredibly ambitious goal to want to become a successful artist – considering how few actually make it. But only those who set themselves ambitious goals and believe in them will achieve anything. It's better to think too big; you can always go smaller if necessary.
You don't always have to tell everyone about your big goals, especially not in the art world, where it will rarely make you any friends. Furthermore, there are cultures where announcing your big goals isn't the proper thing to do and understatement is the way to go. Nevertheless, you have to set goals and live by them.

If you become successful as an artist, there will come a time when you will have to think professionally and on a larger scale very quickly. Only those who can think big can later act big when needed and meet the new requirements.

Don't let little things get in the way. You should realize that that's what they are – just small problems – and you must take care of them as soon as possible, before they become big problems.

7.5. You have no chance alone!

"You need friends and allies! You reach the top together. Not alone!"

As you should have learned by now, the art world is a very complex construct. You can't become a successful artist all by yourself. You need people who will help you and support you in your development.

Seek out people in the art world who have similar goals and ideas as you and accompany one another on parts of the journey. This makes many things easier. You benefit from each other, increase your endurance, and can have a greater impact. Some will accompany you only a little way, others the whole way, until the end. Take advantage of common interests. If your goals diverge, you should both look for new companions.

7.6. Put your ego away!

"If you want success, you have to be willing to eat dirt."

If you think you're the most awesome artist ever, that's totally okay. However, if it's beneath you to eat dirt to become successful, then forget it. Your pride, your honor, your ego, even your dignity, must sometimes be set aside – without traumatizing yourself, of course.

You're allowed to be eccentric, you're allowed to stand out. You can move in certain elite circles, but never put your ego before your art!

Enjoy the privileges and freedom of action you are granted as an artist. But don't forget, in reality the world keeps turning even without art and the art system. Don't take yourself so seriously!

"The world wasn't waiting for you, and for the time being, it's not interested in you, either."

Maybe your art isn't always the most important factor? Maybe you were chosen for an exhibition because of your gender, your background, your skin color, or whatever, to fulfill a quota? If this is completely repugnant to you and you want to rebel against this type of decision, then that's understandable and you can do that. Otherwise, forget your ego, just accept it, use your current advantage, and do something sustainable for your art career.

7.7. Invest in your art career!

"Invest in your art, not your well-being or comfort."

Invest in your art and in your career. In other words: Invest in materials, your workplace and tools, education, networking, and external manpower. You can often save money relatively easily by adjusting your standard of living. Lead a spartan life.

Tools enable and facilitate your work. Tools include not only brushes or hammers, but also your laptop and cell phone. Today, they are indispensable and essential for working professionally. Good tools last much longer and professional ones make your work easier. Theoretically, you can manage your entire career with a good smartphone these days.

Attending relevant art events is important for your education, and also for networking. Invest in such trips.

If you urgently need a good text or a website and you can't do it yourself or through friends, then get it done for money.

Investing does not mean spending money senselessly! Always weigh up your investments well and consider other options.

7.8. Be a networker!

"Being connected is the be-all and end-all of the art world."

Who you know usually determines where you are exhibited, and where you are exhibited determines how relevant you are in the artistic canon and, accordingly, in the art system. Almost everything works via connections. Accept it or become an amateur artist! Use your network both ways, get help and help others.

You need to gain access to the art system and art network and continually expand it through more relevant contacts.

Be a networker in places where people and institutions relevant to the art system are concentrated. Depending on how far along you are in your career, other contacts are interesting for you and vice versa. Remember, you also have to be able to offer people something that appeals to them, or they won't be interested in you. As a young student, for example, you can at most prepare a contact with a museum director. You can only really activate it when you can demonstrate notable successes and have risen to a league that interests him or her.

If you are an introvert, force yourself to go to exhibitions. If you are an extrovert, force yourself to stay in the studio and work.

Go to relevant openings and art events in your area regularly. Find one or two friends in the art world who are also ambitious and who will go with you. This also makes it easier if you feel unsure at first. Look for the interesting people there. Learn to analyze societies. Talk casually but also approach certain people specifically. Grow your network. You are here to work and not for pleasure.

Always be ready to share something exciting about you and your art. Exchange contact details. It doesn't matter whether you use social media, e-mail, or business cards to do this. The important thing is that you also get the other person's contact details and can therefore send him or her information. Business cards still make a professional impression. Linking through social media is sometimes more straightforward. It is recommended to always have both available.

Not only do you have to acquire new contacts, you also have to cultivate the ones you have.

It is advisable to know who's who in the art scene – not so you can address people specifically, but so you can assess the value of an art event.

Opening your own alternative artist-run space with friends can – if ambitiously managed – be an easy and quick way to connect in the local art system and make helpful contacts. However, such projects are also very time-consuming and you must always consider whether it's worth the effort and whether the timing is right.

"Over the years, you get to know a lot of people and scatter seeds everywhere. It's worth it. You'll harvest the crop later. Remember – it's a small world. Today someone may be unimportant and tomorrow that person may be on the panel of whatever award you're applying for."

"But networking alone won't help you. There are thousands of artists who only network but don't work hard."

7.9. Reflect on yourself regularly!

"Only those who regularly check their position can keep their feet on the ground."

You need to keep questioning yourself and your actions to a healthy degree, without fueling self-doubt or giving in to hubris.

Ask yourself questions: How far have you actually come in the last few years? Is anyone interested in what you do? Are you still in the right city? What are your next steps? Who and what is holding you back from success? How can you overcome these obstacles? And so on.

A healthy self-assessment will help you see where you may have lost your way or set goals that you cannot achieve with your current strategy and resources. Accordingly, you need to make decisions that will get you back on track. Be optimistic, yet realistic. Always try to view and evaluate your work and career objectively.

Opinions of other people are an important tool for self-reflection, but you must always consider what their own interests are in relation to you and how knowledgeable they really are.

7.10. Professionalism please!

"Professionalism please!"

Think of being an artist as a profession like others – and a profession requires professionalism. Reliability and a sense of duty are paramount here. Keep your word. Complete everything in a timely manner, including reading and replying to e-mails. Always confirm agreements briefly by e-mail, even if others feel it is superfluous.

In the art world there are rules, conventions, and business practices. You have learned of many of them in this book, and you'll encounter others throughout your career. It is worth noting that some are difficult to understand, especially for young artists. Accept them anyway for now. Everything else is just unprofessional and exhausting for your "business partners."

Upstanding loyalty is a basis for successful, sustainable cooperation and can make many things easier, but blind loyalty is not advisable. Loyalty can no longer be taken for granted, and it must be earned by all involved. Remember, a bad reputation makes the rounds in the small art world faster than you think.

Never promise too much. If your gallery asks for ten new works for your next solo show, but you're worried about the timeframe, promise only eight that you can deliver in top quality. And if there is time, surprise the gallery with two more.

Until you've worked with Zwirner, Gagosian, or Serpentine, or exhibited at MoMA or the Venice Biennales, it's imperative that your name and contact details can be found via Google – even if it's just through a simple website with your e-mail address or social media.

The international art world is English-speaking and computer skills are a must!

"Another tip: There is an infinite amount of knowledge in the field of art. And there are many people who believe they have internalized all of it. Don't be one of those know-it-alls who end up knowing too little."

7.11. The eleventh commandment

No one should take all knowledge of the art world as absolute, because it's a world constructed by humans. Even these commandments are not laws of nature and everything changes. If you want to establish yourself in the art world, you must always align yourself with the system, which is subject to change.

Question what others claim. Form your own opinion, including about the advice in this book. This does not mean that you necessarily have to come to a different conclusion, but it means you have followed the train of thought yourself and not blindly adopted it.

"Take a break and think. That's also important for your art."

8. Factors and strategies for success

"What separates a successful artist from a failed artist is the will to persevere."

As already proven in a study published in the prestigious magazine "Science" in November 2018 in an article entitled "Quantifying reputation and success in art," an artist's career is neither solely dependent on the way of creating art, nor does it happen randomly. This chapter explains, in an easy-to-understand way and with practical examples, what success depends on and what brings it within reach of the artist.

The following are all the factors that significantly influence the success of an artist. Together, they determine your chances of success. Most of the factors have already been mentioned in the book. They are now listed here concisely to once again clarify the interrelationships in the art system.

Furthermore, strategies will be outlined that have enabled success in the art system to date.

8.1. Factors

The factors are listed below in order of importance and weighting. First of all, contacts are the most important and have the most influence on your success as an artist. The further down the list the factors are, the less influential they are. Some factors you can influence, others you cannot, and then there are factors that you can only influence with great effort.

In the end, the overall score determines how great your chances are of a successful career as an artist, but keep in mind that not all factors are weighted equally. Disadvantages in certain factors can be compensated by other factors. Of course, however, the factors must dovetail to the right degree in order to have an effect.

To state it once again in all clarity: These factors are absolutely crucial, and you can tell from them very specifically whether you even meet the requirements for a successful career as an artist.

Using examples and with the corresponding scores, you can check for yourself whether the factors seem favorable or unfavorable for you personally. Go through the list from top to bottom and assess your initial situation using scores.

The grades are:
1 = very good, 2 = good, 3 = satisfactory, 4 = sufficient, 5 = poor, 6 = insufficient

Contacts

Contacts are the be-all and end-all for you. Many things function through recommendations. They can get you exhibitions, put you in touch with galleries, and so on.

Who do you know in the art world?

If you're good friends with the curator of the local art museum, that's classed as satisfactory. But if you are close friends with an international curator such as Hans Ulrich Obrist, then of course that is classed as very good.

Assets/money

Money is necessary for survival and – used wisely – can compensate for many factors. And it can open a door or two.

How much money can you spend each month?

If you can cover your living expenses plus a few materials, then that's classed as sufficient. If your fixed costs are covered and you have $10,000 or more at your disposal every month, then that's classed between good and very good.

Time

Time is, of course, the basis of any activity in life.

How much time can you devote to your art career each week?

Seventeen hours is just about sufficient, 70 hours or more is very good.

Career to date

Many players in the art system today rely heavily on an artist's résumé to evaluate him or her.

Where are you studying or where did you study? What residencies, awards, exhibitions, and so on are included on your résumé? And how relevant are they? How well have you optimized your résumé?

Ambition

Ambition drives every career.

How ambitious are you? Are you ready to give everything for your art career?

Are you satisfied if you have an exhibition at the local branch of a bank? This is classed as insufficient. But if you want to go to MoMA and you're really willing to give it your all, that's classed as very good.

Where you live and work

Not every place of residence and work offers the same optimal conditions for participating in the art system.

Are you in a hip metropolis or in a shack somewhere in the boonies?

Paris, Rome, Madrid, Zürich, and Shanghai are classed as sufficient; Berlin and Los Angeles are satisfactory; London is good; New York is very good.

Smartness

As an artist, you need to know the interrelationships in the art system. Many decisions in your career require a clear mind and goal-oriented action.

How smart are you? How well do you know the art system? How awake is your spirit? How well can you see interrelationships? How good are you with money?

Perseverance

A successful career as an artist doesn't happen overnight. You have to develop artistically, you have to build up a network, and so on. All that takes a lot of time and energy.

How persevering are you? How quickly do you give up? Can you also overcome dry spells? How well can you manage setbacks?

Diligence

Producing art is essential and the more hard-working you are, the better. But diligence is not only required in the studio.

How hard do you work in the studio, but also on your art career in general? Do you really make the most of every minute you work and tackle your tasks with ambition?

Luck

Luck is part of life and must not be left out of your career.

Are you someone no one wants to play dice with because you always win? Can you more or less rely on fortune always being on your side?

Age

No one takes you seriously when you're 20, and after 35 you're already ready for the scrap heap, assuming you haven't had a breakthrough yet. If you are 25 years old and have finished your art studies, that's classed as very good. If you are 45 years old without having made the breakthrough, that is classed as poor.

Your artistic work

This is about your artistic work itself.

In which medium do you work? Are the contents and statements of your art in demand right now?

If you work only with a lot of dedication, but without reference to the art world most of the time, that's insufficient. However, if your work is contemporary and clearly located in the artistic canon, that's very good.

Demeanor

Artists are not only defined by their art; their demeanor and social interactions also significantly determine how they are perceived in the art system. How charismatic are you? How good are your people skills? Are you convincing as an exciting artistic personality?

Environment

The social and professional environment in which you operate is crucial for your mindset.

Do you move mainly in the art system? How much time do you spend with people from the professional art system?

Family

Your family is the first possible means of support. In the best case, it can support you financially and open doors for you through contacts. But it can also be a hindrance or irrelevant to your career.

How much can you benefit from your family in terms of your art career? Through money, education, or reputation?

Citizenship and multiculturalism

If you are at home in two or more cultures or countries, you will, in a best-case scenario, have the opportunity to advance your career in more than one place. What's more, internationality is fashionable these days. How good or bad the connection to the global art system is depends on where you are positioned.

Do your multiculturalism and citizenship or your multiple citizenships help you get additional funding or other advantages in the art system? Can you participate in the current trend of multicultural artists where you live and work?

Gender, ethnicity, and so on

In fact, even these artist attributes are always subject to trends. White Christian heterosexual men are not in vogue right now. Everything else is definitely more beneficial at the moment.

You need factors that are in your favor, but you also need to choose a strategy. The strategy is the elevator, while the factors determine whether the elevator stops at your floor and takes you up – or not.

8.2. Strategies

"People think if you're good, you'll be successful and famous. But that's not enough."

Many artists are successful and/or famous, but not actually good artists. Their artistic work can be described as neither good nor sustainable. Nevertheless, they have earned their place in the art world and that deserves respect. They have achieved success with the help of conscious and subconscious decisions and strategies. Check out how other contemporary artists have jump-started their careers.

Below are some proven strategies and considerations that can help your success or partial success. You may realize that you are unknowingly using one or more of these strategies already. With this knowledge, you can now optimize them according to the rules of the art system and use them in a targeted manner. Most strategies can be combined, of course, and it makes sense to do so.

Toward the end of your studies, you have the opportunity to jump on the fast train to success. A few months after graduation at the latest, this opportunity will have passed. To catch that train, however, you have to get into position halfway through your art studies. You should now make purposeful decisions in all areas and proceed by behaving professionally. The likelihood of catching this fast train is very low, and yet it will probably be your biggest and best chance of success in your career as an artist.

You should ask others for advice on how to advance your career, but in the end, you must make the decision yourself, with a clear mind and so that it makes sense to you. Always keep an overview of your artist career. Let other people help you, form purposeful partnerships, but keep the reins in your own hands as much as possible without causing others to distrust you. Learn who you can rely on.

Grow with your generation

Today, one generation is at the helm. Tomorrow, it will be your generation. Grow together with your friends, acquaintances, and business partners. Cultivate and use the contacts of your generation.

Example: The gallery is unknown, you are unknown, you start working together and together you grow and become relevant.

"You think la famiglia of the art world is impenetrable? Eventually, your generation will be good to go, and then it will be your famiglia."

Form a group

Form an interest group of two or more ambitious and hardworking friends from the art world who do good work and, like you, want to become successful. Don't think of yourselves as competitors, think of yourselves as a team. Through mutual support and loyalty, you'll move forward more easily and stand out from the crowd. You can balance out your strengths and weaknesses. You can save time and share resources. Nevertheless, don't give up on yourself for the sake of others.

Basically, only one person needs to become successful and he or she can then pull the others along thanks to his or her contacts and recommendations.

Be the wolf in sheep's clothing

You should be confident, you should be determined, but don't show it to everyone. Very often artists who strongly propagate their own success are ignored by professors, jurors, curators, and so on – not because they are not as good, but because they appear too self-confident. In Europe in particular, the pursuit of personal success is poorly regarded.
There is evidence that a reserved appearance usually has a positive effect on an artist's career in its infancy. But don't be shy or clueless either, your skills must remain clearly visible!

If you are too self-confident, you will miss all the important and necessary funding opportunities, because people will think that you can achieve your goals by yourself and do not need their support and sympathy. Some people want to support artists who wouldn't make it without support. For example, there are jurors and curators who prefer to fund or invite artists where they can make a difference.

"Your goal should not be to be noticed by as many people as possible, but to be noticed by the right and important people."

Always consider group dynamics, too: If, for example, you are part of a group in your studies or elsewhere on which you are unfortunately dependent, too much outward ambition can cause envy and exclude you. Envious people will target you right from the start and put obstacles in your way, even before you have achieved effective success.

Get professional help

Get advice and learn lessons from established players in the art system. Try to maintain the professional contacts you made at art school.

"Investing in professional help will prove to be an advantage."

Through very specific tasks on your part, you can come into contact with established players in the art system to whom you would otherwise not have access. They can perform your tasks professionally, giving you an edge over your peers – and this approach can give you other advantages, too. So if you, as an unknown artist, get someone established from the art world (for example, an art journalist, an experienced artist, etc.) to help you – which of course is not always free of charge – then it may be the case that people not only help you once, but remember you and suggest you another time, for example, for an exhibition, a prize, an article, and so on. At least they know your name now.

Remember, no one runs someone else's business for free just because the other person doesn't feel up to it.

A strong business partner

"Increase the probabilities. When you go fishing, go where there are lots of fish."

Basically you can say: Strong business partners, such as outstanding, highly successful gallery owners, art dealers, or collectors, usually find you – you don't find them. But you can increase your chances of getting noticed. You can go where there are many of these strong business partners. You can expand your network all the way to them. However, certain conditions must be met for them to consider you interesting and suitable. If a strong partner should present himself or herself to you, then this is a stroke of luck that you should probably take advantage of. However, if a collaboration comes about, you must also be able to deliver.

Find a mentor

Mentors are, for example, experienced and sometimes influential professors, artists, curators, or critics who, usually out of personal affinity, can support and encourage you with words and deeds and thus advance your career. If they are not within your sphere through your current contacts, such as your family, then you will have to earn their sympathy and willingness to support you. This is how you develop a personal relationship with each other. They accompany you on your artistic journey for a while, sometimes for their whole life. Most of the time, you will even be genuine friends.

Start off rich

A possible approach may also be to start or advance your art career with a lot of money, either earned elsewhere or available to you through family, for instance. Money allows you to create optimal conditions, be it for your workplace, for art production or for networking, PR, and so on. However, money alone is not enough, it must also be invested strategically and wisely.

"You can easily blow $200,000 in a year without having taken a single step forward in your art career."

Do not rush

"All in good time."

Be goal-oriented, but don't rush into anything. Many young artists want an exhibition as quickly as possible and absolutely want to be represented by a gallery, expecting fame and money. But success does not come with just any exhibitions and any galleries, but only with the good and suitable ones.

What does an exhibition give you at this point in time, besides self-affirmation? Do you really need this affirmation or can you get it in an easier way and with less time and energy? Do you actually already meet the requirements to work with a gallery?

Think about what steps to take and when. Don't waste your time unnecessarily. Be daring. Still, check to see if you already meet the requirements for your next goal. And ask yourself if it's important for your career, or if it just satisfies your ego.

Keep in mind, few of the really good opportunities in an art career come spontaneously. Spontaneous things are usually short-lived and organized by people who are inconsistent and often act erratically. In the longer term, this type of collaboration is rarely fruitful.

For the more advanced: diversify

Often, artists establish themselves as either market artists or biennale artists. But the truly sustainable careers are those in which artists either manage the balancing act between the two, or make a concerted effort after the fact to establish themselves in the other field as well. To do this, it is usually also necessary to expand their artistic practice, whether formally or in terms of content.

One example is Oscar Murillo. Initially the epitome of the young market artist, he has managed – with the help of his business partners – to additionally establish himself as a political and biennale artist, which has cemented his place in art history.

9. Practical knowledge

"Trust is good, control is better, and don't mix money and friendship."

At this point, topics that have already been touched upon in part will be dealt with in greater depth, and others that could not be suitably accommodated elsewhere in the book will be examined. Furthermore, some practical questions that arise in the everyday life of an artist will be answered.

9.1. Exhibiting

It doesn't matter how many exhibitions you have, it matters how high quality and how relevant the exhibitions you participate in are. Strong exhibition practice will give you experience, but it is not essential to become successful. More central, perhaps, is the ability to meet deadlines in order to complete works and groups of works in time for planned exhibitions. Nevertheless, there are of course disciplines, such as performance and installations, where exhibitions are often one of the few opportunities for the works to become art, and strong exhibition practice is beneficial here.

Whether an exhibition is relevant is determined primarily by the exhibition venue and the curator, sometimes also by the context, for example, in the case of an exhibition or an art award specifically showcasing and supporting emerging artists. How established are the venue, curator, and award? In which circles are they established and in which league do they play? Alternative spaces, for instance, are rarely places where artists are actually discovered. Nevertheless, exhibitions can give you helpful feedback on your art, provided you also want to listen and aren't just there for the attention and for your ego.

It's important to develop a sense of how your work will look outside of your studio. One can argue whether the white cube – that is, white, neutral space – is the measure of all exhibition spaces. Whatever, exhibition spaces today usually have in common that they want to focus on the artworks in the best possible way and give them enough room. An exhibition space therefore allows you to view your work in a neutral and "professional" way, in contrast to your probably cramped and visually distracting studio.

A big benefit of exhibitions in general is being able to nurture your following, let them know you're still on the ball, and offer them the opportunity to see new works from you. You can intensify contacts and also make new ones.

In the exhibition business, a distinction is made between two types of exhibition: the solo show or solo exhibition and the group show or group exhibition. In a solo exhibition, as the name suggests, the focus is on just one artist. In the group exhibition, several artists exhibit together. The solo exhibition is more prestigious for you, but in a group exhibition you can benefit as an artist from the reputation of the other participants. Constructs such as "double solo exhibitions/two-person exhibitions" have also become established. Here, two artists are shown at the same time, but usually in separate rooms; only one opening takes place.

Promote exhibitions and establish contacts

If you have an exhibition, the work isn't finished once you have completed the presentation. You should promote the exhibition in advance and during it through all channels – in your personal newsletter, on invitation cards, via social media, and so on.

A professional press kit enables you or the exhibition team to promote the exhibition in the media, both print and digital. Basically, it's mainly the trade press that is relevant for you as an artist. Nevertheless, reports in the feuilleton/art section or weekend issues of the high-quality daily press can also support your career in the long term. In the digital realm, in addition to the websites of established print media, it is art blogs, getting featured on Instagram, and so on that can have a very far-reaching influence these days. If you did not organize the exhibition yourself and your host fails to inform the media, you should do it yourself and professionally after the opening and in consultation with the host.

You should also keep a close eye on who is interested in your art at the opening, for example, so that you can stay in touch with them. If your exhibition is at a gallery, let the gallery owner do the work and don't get in his or her way. Nevertheless, you should always take an active role, not a passive one.

Document your exhibitions

"An exhibition that is not documented is an exhibition that did not happen."

Ensure your exhibitions are properly and well documented with photos and/or videos. If necessary, pay someone to do this for you! Remember: Invest in your career! In addition to the need for documentation, the exhibition offers you an optimal opportunity to photograph/document your work in a representative and professional manner, giving you the opportunity to gain perfect source material for a high-quality portfolio.

Getting paid for exhibiting

Basically, participation in exhibitions that are of interest to you is either free of charge or you receive expenses. There are other models, but they are mainly aimed at amateur artists. In exhibitions among artist friends, it is customary to share the costs fairly between all participants.

Whether expenses can be paid and what they cover depends largely on how much funding the exhibition venue is given. It is by no means a matter of course that there is any payment for participation in an exhibition. Please note, however: Renowned and thus often relevant exhibition spaces are usually supported by private and public funding, and the artist is often provided with lump-sum expenses.

Museums and established institutions typically do not pay fees to the artist, but will cover transportation and insurance costs and pay expenses or a production fee, as appropriate. The amount is individual, but usually rather modest for young artists. Remember: The artist benefits from the reputation of the institution, which is theoretically worth many times more than mere money. If necessary, however, there are various ways in which the institution and the artist can obtain additional production budget, be it through funding programs, galleries, foundations, collectors, and so on.

Art school as an opportunity

In most art schools, there are regular public occasions when students can present their work, usually directly in the school buildings. The requirements for participation vary from school to school. At some, all students are allowed to participate, while at others, you must qualify. These events have names such as open studios, annual (student) exhibition, annual presentation, open day, open house, tour, first year exhibition, and so on.

In some places, art school exhibitions are considered of little importance by students, as well as professors. While such an exhibition does not look exciting on your résumé, experience has shown that more artists are discovered at such exhibitions than elsewhere. The audience is often interspersed with a few high-profile individuals who make these exhibitions much more valuable than most others you will have at a young age and consider more important. It would be desirable if all art schools recognized and expanded the great potential of these presentations.

Take advantage of these opportunities at your art school. It is often noted that many of the exhibiting young artists are not present in person. Again: Professionalism please!

Be present on all days for the full day, even if it is very exhausting and your fellow students show much less presence in comparison. Be prepared to give information about your work. Know the prices of your artworks in advance. Offer fair and realistic prices. Have a portfolio printed out or ready on a tablet. Have business cards on hand. If someone wants your contact details, ask them to give you theirs too. That's the only way you will be able to write to them later if they don't get back to you. Analyze people: Which ones want to talk to you because they just have a need to say something and which ones really know about art and are interested in your work? As a basic rule of thumb: Out of the thousand people who come along, between one and three really matter and can help you get ahead. They don't register in advance and you'll miss them if you're not paying attention. You need to be active, because they often aren't. Reach out to people you think or know are important. This mindset will help you in the future, after art school. If you are struggling to complete these tasks, team up with a colleague and motivate each other to get the most out of the situation.

Building this mindset is important so that by the time your graduate show comes around at the latest, you'll be perfectly practiced and able to pull out all the stops. It will be the last opportunity for you to get important and good contacts with comparatively little effort and hopefully initiate the next steps in your career. If you don't, it will be hard work.

9.2. Selling

When selling your art, your goal should be less about wanting to make money with it and more about using it to further your art career. Sales prove that people value your art so much that they are willing to spend hundreds or even thousands of dollars on it. Sales are thus also evidence of a promising artist, giving him or her more legitimacy, and should not be reduced to their function as a source of income.

This chapter is therefore not primarily about explaining *how* to sell your art. Rather, it will give you some helpful hints associated with selling your work. Furthermore, it will make you aware that sales support your career on a number of levels, which will be elaborated on in more depth in a later chapter.

Nevertheless, here are a few words about the money you will receive when you sell your works. This is to be invested specifically in your art and career, until you get to where you want to be. Money can positively influence and advance your artistic work, making it more in volume, bigger, better, more detailed, more colorful, faster, easier, and so on. It also gives you many more options: You can commission professional texts, photos, PR, and so on for yourself, use it to pay for your plane ticket to visit the Biennale, buy the right tools, and more.

"You can sell as many paintings as you want directly from your studio to your relatives and make a living, but beyond that it's not going to get you very far in your career as an artist."

If your art is offered for sale and someone buys one or more of your works, it is important to analyze and classify this sales process in order to draw conclusions for your career.

So ask yourself questions such as: Who buys and with what motivation? At what price and how many works? And how did the sale come about? More specifically: Is the buyer a professional and a regular in the business (in other words, an art collector, dealer, or the like) or a one-off purchaser (a private individual) or perhaps something in between? And at what price did he or she buy the work? This can tell you how exciting you are to which audience and how your art is valued by them.

At which occasion did the sale happen? During an exhibition at art school, in an alternative space or gallery, or at an art fair? Are sales common in these contexts? Are sales necessary to keep the venue running? What are the average prices and sales? Who was involved in the closing of the sale? Was there a recommendation?

Furthermore, it's important to always ask yourself: Why is the purchase being made now? Is it because you have an exhibition at a gallery right now? Is it because of an article in a magazine? Is it because your prices are relatively low at the moment? Or because you just won a prize or an award?

All the answers to these questions can give you important clues to assess your situation and show you how influential certain players, events, and measures can be.

In principle, art can be sold at all exhibitions. In a gallery, this is obvious. In a contemporary museum, it is more discreet. As mentioned at the beginning, art is even sold at the Venice Biennale. What may seem strange to some has long been common in the art world and is only to your advantage.

The following deals are common: alternative space, artist-run space, etc.: 20%–50% sales commission, museum: 10%–20% sales commission, gallery: 50% sales commission.

What to give away, what to keep

"Your works are your best advertisement. Send your babies on their way, let them tell everyone about you."

On the one hand, your works are your best advertisement in the world out there. Don't hoard your artwork in your studio at all costs. Let them circulate!

If you have enough works for future exhibitions, it's okay to sell a work below price if you are forced to do so. Pride rarely gets you anywhere, but the money you earn can be invested in materials and your career, so it can serve you well.

On the other hand, you should regularly hold back some outstanding works, provided you work hard to produce more. You can always use these works for prestigious exhibitions or sell them specifically to good collections at a much later date.

The buyer is usually your friend

A little story: "Many a young artist sees art buyers as adversaries who push the price down at the time of purchase in order to profit later on from an enormous increase in value and to be able to sell at a high price. They do not care about the content of the art. They speculate only as greedy capitalist swines in the art market and take all the works they acquire as quickly as possible to the gloomy tomb of the bonded warehouse, while the half-starved artist looks on sadly."

Indeed, there are rotten apples everywhere, including among art buyers, but artists rarely encounter them at the beginning of their career.

Basically, you have to consider that a buyer of works by an unknown artist is taking a high financial risk. After all, statistically speaking, over 90% of artists do not become superstars and the works do not increase in value. On the contrary, much of it will be completely worthless later on.

Most art buyers are also very cooperative later on and often you can call them without any problems and ask if you can borrow the sold work for a few months for an important exhibition. After all, they profit from it too.

And, should a buyer really be able to sell your work for a very high price, then you are probably already rich enough and, considering the risk the buyer took at the time, it's perfectly okay that he or she gets to pocket the profit and you should be happy about the joint success story.

However, you should still consider and understand a few important things:

If someone owns some or many of your works, they can automatically influence your career, both positively and negatively.

If your career is successful and you sell regularly, it is very likely that sooner or later works of yours will end up on the secondary art market. Then, works can turn out to be boomerangs, having gone, for example, to buyers who mainly speculate in art and now want to rake in profits. Or they may go to respected art collectors who might go bankrupt because of a stock market crash or drop dead overnight. Their collection is then auctioned off. This too can unintentionally influence your career. If the market cannot absorb the works now on offer, your prices will drop. However, you have the option of not leaving this to chance. You can always intervene in the secondary market yourself or with the help of a partner (gallery, dealer, collector) and thus guarantee stable sales prices. Whether you will be provided with the necessary capital is, of course, another question. If your career might otherwise end abruptly, an intervention is probably worthwhile.

That's why it is advisable not to sell blindly to everyone. Concentrations of multiple works should be in good hands and, as your career progresses, the secondary market must be kept in mind. With all these things, an experienced and professional gallery can prove to be very helpful.

Pricing

As a rule, you determine the prices of your works yourself. If you work with business partners – such as a gallery – you can also hand over pricing to them. In each case, of course, they must give their consent to your prices, but it is often a collaborative process.

To determine the prices of two-dimensional artworks, in particular paintings, you can use the principle of:

$$(\text{height} + \text{width}) \times \text{factor } X = \text{net sales price}$$

This method is often used by artists, but also gallery owners, as a guideline. You add the height of your work in centimeters/inches to the width in centimeters/inches. Then you multiply this sum by X. X is, for example, 10 (if you use centimeters) or 25.4 (if you use inches) and depends on the price range of your works and how successful you are. Sales taxes are then added to that amount. For example, if an artist paints in different formats, this allows easy adaptation of prices and prevents discussions. The X factor is increased with increasing popularity.

Conversely, you can take the price excluding sales tax of a work, divide it by the sum of height and width, and get the factor of an artist. In this way, you can easily find out where others have set their prices and orientate yourself accordingly.

However, you should by no means take the formula as absolute, it is only a tool that helps you with realistic pricing, and is very useful especially at the beginning of your career, when you do not yet have a feeling for prices. It also has "weaknesses", such as the property of valuing a large painting as less valuable than two smaller works that, taken together, have the same surface area. Consequently, as your career progresses, large paintings may need to have a higher factor than small paintings. In addition, not all your work will necessarily have the same factor, because some may be technically more complex than others, for example.

If your work is not two-dimensional, there is unfortunately no simple formula that you can use to help. Production costs and production effort play a role here, but ultimately you just have to base your estimates on feeling. But here too, the development of your prices must be justified and logical.

An artist's pricing policy is much more important and has more impact on an artist's career than many people think. If you have no idea about prices, you are advised to consult experienced people and do research. This way, you can get to know how other and comparable artists are rated during their career and get a feeling for prices accordingly.

If you want to be taken seriously, your prices must not be too low, but also not too high. And they must always be in relation to your current situation and career. If in doubt, it is better to set the prices slightly too low. In principle, you can always increase your prices, but it's not easy to adjust them downwards.

It is possible to serve different price ranges at the same time. In a relatively simple way, this can be done by size, varying complexity, or number of copies in a series. There are more possibilities, too, including lithography, editions, and so on. You therefore have the opportunity to address different customers and make yourself less dependent on one target group.

"Pay attention to local specifics. In China, for example, don't include the number 4, but do include the number 8 in your prices."

Haggling is nothing unusual in the sale of art. After all, the prices are basically nonmaterial. Buyers will try to push your selling price down to a greater or lesser extent, depending on the setting (studio sale, gallery sale, etc.) in which you are selling. Furthermore, the more prestigious the buyer, collection, or institution, the more discount may also be justified. For example, if a gallery sells a work into a good collection, a 20% discount is not uncommon.

Agreements

Many things in the art business are done on a basis of trust. Nevertheless, it is advisable to put as much as possible in writing. Nowadays, it's easy to do this by e-mail.
If you work with a gallery, you should insist on an art consignment agreement. For less professional sales exhibitions, an e-mail with the amount of the commission and a list of works with the sales prices will

also suffice – after all, you don't want to bother the organizers with paperwork and you might make yourself unpopular. Make it clear in your mail whether the prices include commission and taxes or not.

Basically, you should give your business partners as few opportunities as possible to cheat on you without making them think you mistrust them. Always handle financial matters promptly and in writing only, if possible.

Studio sales

If you don't have a gallery (or another partner to represent you in business), you can of course sell your work from your studio. If you have a gallery, it is advisable to sell your work through the gallery. First, it makes a professional impression; second, it builds trust with your gallery; third, it helps you support them financially, which in turn benefits you because it allows them to invest in your career. If the customers know your name or the work through the gallery, move in the same circles as the gallery, are customers of the gallery, or come from the same city as the gallery, or similar, you must never bypass the gallery.
Sales prices of works sold directly from your studio should not differ or differ only marginally from the "official" prices. Don't create incentives for bargain hunters.

Studio sales should not be a long-term strategy. As an amateur artist or local artist, you might be able to survive financially, but you have little chance of establishing yourself as a relevant artist beyond the region.

Commissions

There are always artists who feel insulted when they are asked about a commission. Yet, commissioned art is one of the origins of our current art business and is much more widespread than some think.

In principle, everyone must decide for themselves whether and under what conditions they take on commissions. However, you should not disregard the fact that payment is usually good and you might develop a lasting friendship with the client.

If the client expects the work to be produced under your name as an artist, you must, of course, meet your own standards of quality, concept, and aesthetics.

See also chapter 9.5. "Accepting commissions."

Signature, certificate, editions

Your work must be visibly signed with your signature somewhere – on the front or back or wherever. If this is not the case, an additional certificate with your signature, and preferably with an image, must be attached. As a rule, artists sign with their signature and year/date. Including further details – such as the full name of the artist and title of the work – somewhere on the work is very useful. The place of origin can also be added.

For example, if you make conceptual or ephemeral art, you usually sell a certificate that allows its restaging/reenactment, that is, instructions on how to do so and your signature. At its most simple, this can be a handwritten sheet of paper.

If the same work exists more than once, it is usually referred to as an edition. Numbers must be added to these works. For example, 1/7 + 2 AP means this is work number one of seven copies and there are two additional copies for the artist personally. AP here stands for "artist's proof" and is not officially meant for sale.

As a general rule, in the case of works that are easy to reproduce or works with certificates, it is advisable either to note the edition or to use the word "unique" in order to make clear that this is either a limited multiple work or a single work, and thus exclude misunderstandings or misuse.

Sold-out editions can generally be produced again relatively easily, for example by adjusting the format a little. Well-known artists often like to use this tactic. Whether this is cheating is another matter. Where there is demand, there is also supply.

Some terms

Tax

Taxes, including value-added tax (VAT) also known as sales tax.

In most countries, the sale of all tangible goods is taxed.

Artists are usually exempt in their early days because they have too few sales, but galleries generally have to pay tax and therefore sell your works with the addition of sales tax.

Sales price

This is the price that the end customer has to pay. To avoid misunderstandings, it is always advisable to specify whether the price includes sales tax or not. If you don't know, say it's the net price – in other words, the price without sales tax. That way, you're on the safe side.

Sales commission

If someone else (for example, a gallery) sells your works for you, they are entitled to a previously agreed share of the sales price. If the commission is 50% and the selling price for your work is $1,000 excluding sales tax, the seller will receive $500 commission.

Insured value

In most cases, the insured value means the current market value. In other words, the average price that is currently paid for the work of art on the market. Young artists often do not yet have an established market value and so the insurance value is usually equated with the production costs. This means: How much would your work cost to produce if you added up the cost of materials, etc., and paid yourself an hourly wage for a reasonable amount of time invested? Ultimately, of course, the determination of the insured value of a work depends on the individual handling and budget of the exhibition organizer.

Art flipping

Perhaps writing about art flipping (basically the speculative buying and selling of art) here is taking things a little too far, because the chances that it could affect you are almost zero. Nevertheless, it is worth touching on the subject, because it fascinates many young artists.

Art flipping is both a curse and a blessing. Not every artist and all works are automatically suitable for art flipping. If you fit the art flipper's prey pattern, you often can't influence whether you will become their target.

As soon as you become a voluntary or involuntary target of art flipping, you need strong and reliable partners (a gallery, collectors, and so on) otherwise your demise will come as quickly as your success. Whatever, it certainly remains highly risky for you.

There is no 100% protection against unwanted art flipping, but consistently using the "know your customer" principle helps a lot. Who buys my works and how many works do they have of mine? The same applies to your gallery or galleries, of course.

9.3. Working with a gallery

Galleries have been an integral part of the art system for decades and are intimately familiar with how an artist's work accumulates value. This means you, as an artist, can focus primarily on your art while the gallery advances your business and career. This is, of course, the ideal situation and it doesn't exactly happen like this in real life. Nevertheless, a gallery is an important and helpful partner in establishing yourself more firmly in the art system.

All artists, including biennale artists, should consider working with a gallery. However, the right time comes sooner for some than for others.

Requirements

In order to work successfully with a gallery, certain requirements must be met. Your work should be tangible or materializable in some way and thus sellable. It must have a certain maturity and quality. There must be a guaranteed minimum number of works available. There must be evidence of continuity in your production. And, last but not least, you should display maturity as an artistic personality.

If you can't meet these requirements, galleries can't help you with your career for the time being – and they won't be interested in you, either.

For example, if your work is not in itself optimally suited for sale (performance, installation, etc.) and must be converted into another form or a side product must be created from it, you must ask yourself whether it is worth the effort at that moment.

If you think you meet the requirements and the time is right, the next question is: How attractive are you to a gallery? There are other points to consider in this respect: First, the maturity of your artwork is important, and this includes having a common thread running through your work. In addition, your artwork should have a unique selling point and, at best, serve a theme from the current art discourse. And don't forget your résumé, which can be a significant aspect.

Finding a gallery

Next, you should get a detailed picture of the gallery landscape, so you can filter out potential partners. You can find out in advance whether a gallery is a good fit for you by looking at its program and the artists it represents. Do your themes fit the gallery? Do they already have an artist who works in a very similar way to you, which could result in unintentional confusion?

Get an accurate picture of the gallery: How long has the gallery existed? Who is behind the gallery? Where does the money come from? What kind of audience does it attract? What is the price range of the works offered? How enterprising is the gallery? What art fairs does it attend? Who are the other artists? How well known and successful are they? Is it the main gallery of these artists or just a side gallery? How long have they been working together? How regularly do they have solo exhibitions at the gallery? Many of these questions are indicators of the gallery's value and provide insight into its collaboration with its artists.

Ultimately, you can only find out whether the gallery really suits you by meeting one-on-one. And, unfortunately, it often takes months or years of cooperation until you know how professional a gallery really is. It is therefore advisable that you rely on personal recommendations and reports, too.

Next, how do you make contact with galleries? On the one hand, galleries usually turn away young artists, sometimes rudely, because they are unknown and supposedly insignificant. On the other hand, few galleries want to miss a burgeoning superstar. So, the better your hand of cards is, the more likely they are to sit up and take notice. But set realistic goals. Usually, the larger and more established the gallery, the less likely you are to succeed, unless you have a very influential contact directly with the gallery. You have a good chance with gallery owners of your generation, who are more or less your age group.

"The galleries want to discover you! So you shouldn't force yourself on them, but you also have to be sure they can't overlook you, either."

If you're really good, and at the same time you can generate enough attention (through your graduate show, art prizes, grants, shows for emerging artists, exhibitions, etc.), galleries may approach you. If this doesn't happen, you have to try to enter into a dialog with the galleries through your contacts. This can happen during a casual conversation, where someone you know introduces you to the gallery and you ask if you can show them your portfolio. Alternatively, it can happen via a specific recommendation. This is usually the most promising option.

Addressing a gallery directly without an intermediary very rarely leads to the desired result – unless your career is already bearing fruit that just needs to be picked. For example, if you have regular sales from your studio and perhaps a great show right now and several requests for sales, you can approach a suitable gallery and ask them if they would be interested in handling these and future sales for you. You will lose about half of the profit, but it is a very elegant way to get into a gallery.

How picky you can be in your gallery search depends on how good your contacts are and how well you meet the above requirements. You shouldn't spend too long looking, because many talented and hungry artists graduate from art schools every year. However, the first gallery is not always the best one. It should fit. As a rule, you are allowed to change to another gallery later. After all, you develop. And remember: Galleries, like artists, exist in very different leagues. For example, if you're too hasty to work with a mediocre gallery, you may prevent yourself from working with other and better galleries.

Rules for collaboration

It's no longer common today for an artist to be under contract with a gallery, especially not gagged in an exclusive agreement. This has advantages and disadvantages: It means more freedom for you, but also more personal responsibility. Many things have become less binding and there is no longer as clear a division of tasks as in the past. This does not make the situation easier for either party.

If the gallery sells works of yours, unless otherwise agreed, 50% of the proceeds of the sale, excluding taxes, will go to the artist, and the gallery will pay for the transportation of the works to and from the exhibition. Usually, your works are also insured.

For cost-intensive productions, you can often claim additionally agreed expenses. Like taxes, these are deducted from the sales price and only then is the amount split. You can then add the expenses to your share of the money later.

For example, if you have to travel for the installation or for the exhibition opening, reasonable travel and accommodation costs can also be paid by galleries. The practice here varies a lot and must be clarified in advance.

If you are properly established, the packing of your works is usually done by a specialized transport company and taken care of by your gallery.

If the gallery has sold a work of yours, you usually have to invoice the gallery for your share. If you are required to pay sales tax, you must add it to your share when you issue your invoice. The gallery should normally transfer the money to your account within four weeks of the sale.

Generally, the gallery can give a 10% discount on the sales price without consulting you. If it gives more discount, it must discuss the matter with you or deduct it from its share.

What specific conditions you can impose in the first years of your career as an artist depends largely on your success, your negotiating skills, and the goodwill of your gallery.

If you plan to cooperate with a gallery and your works will be sold by them, then you must put this in writing in advance in a consignment agreement. This is a list of works with a photo, the dimensions, the title, the date, and the technique/material of each work. The amount (excluding taxes) that each work will be sold for in the gallery is defined here. This is also where the agreements on percentage share/commission, transportation, expenses for production costs, payment modalities, and so on are determined. Furthermore, the consignment agreement specifies a period of "lending." A common duration, for example, is one year. After that, the gallery must either return the work to you, buy it, or conclude a new consignment agreement. The gallery draws up the consignment agreement. You just need to provide all the information. If you work with a gallery, you must always insist on a consignment agreement. No consignment agreement, no exhibition!

Loyalty is frequently an issue when working with galleries. Loyalty is something valuable, but it must come from both parties and stops where one of the parties tries to restrict the other party's freedom to make necessary business decisions. Many forget that both parties can benefit from the other's success. A confident demeanor will help you get the freedom you need.

If buyers deliberately try to bypass your gallery and seek a direct sale from your studio, with the gallery excluded, you must not act on it. The rules for this were already set out in the section on studio sales.

When working with multiple galleries, the basic principle is: You should have no more than one gallery per city and no more than two or three galleries per country working independently of one another.

Galleries can enter into different types of collaborations with each other. These can be suggested by the gallery or the artist. And many kinds of deals are negotiated.

For example, if two galleries clash over a one-time exhibition in the same area, a common solution is to designate the gallery that has represented the artist for a longer period of time and primarily in that area as the main gallery. The latter gets 5–10% of the net sales price if a work of the artist is sold in the second gallery. This commission is deducted from the gallery's percentage. The artist keeps his or her 50%.

Your gallery and you

"The perfect gallery doesn't exist any more than the perfect artist exists."

Each artist is different, and so is each gallery – they all have their varying concepts and approaches. But what they all have in common is that they diversify. This means they have several artists in their portfolio who they manage, and they generate their revenue with all of them together. Among them, of course, there are flagship artists, who carry the other artists along not only financially, but also with their reputation.

Because the gallery represents multiple artists at once, it can't give you the sole attention you may desire. And it can't put all its energy and resources into just one artist. Good galleries may try to make you feel like you're the only artist, but of course the truth is that you aren't.

To what extent you put your career in the hands of a gallery is basically up to you. Some artists have more capacity, while others have less. The independent artist advocated here is advised to stay in control. You always remain responsible for your own career, even when working with a partner.

Try to establish a regular dialog with your gallery. This is not only conducive to a fruitful collaboration, but is also a way to keep them informed about how hard you are working in the studio. It's important that the gallery always keeps you in mind. If possible, visit the gallery occasionally.

Think not only about what the gallery can do for you, but also what you can do for the gallery. For example, do you have good contacts that the gallery could profit from? Do you know collectors you can introduce to the gallery?

Understand that success is achieved together and it usually happens when the gallery and artist work well together.

"What's good for the gallery is good for its artists. And vice versa. People forget that sometimes."

Optimally, both parties will come to the overriding realization that the active use of synergies can have a lasting positive impact beyond a temporary collaboration, if only by boosting reputations, gaining additional experience, or making new contacts on both sides.

"Just because you are represented by a gallery doesn't mean you're going to be shown regularly or taken to art fairs. There are the artists on the bench, too."

Reflect on the collaboration with your gallery: Is the collaboration bringing you what you hoped it would? If not, did you have other expectations? Or is the gallery unsuitable for you? Can you meet the standards of the gallery? And is the gallery up to your standards? Do you expect more support from them? How regularly do they show your works and take you to art fairs? Why have you sold a lot? Why have you sold a little? What has the gallery done to promote you?

If possible, try to understand how your gallery works. Try to compare this knowledge with other galleries to get a deeper understanding of the gallery business in general and your gallery's business in particular. This knowledge will be very useful to you later when you make important decisions. Ask yourself the following questions: How is your gallery financed? How regularly does it sell? Where does it generate its most important sales (the gallery or art fairs)? What kind of customers does it have? And so on.

Always keep an eye on business dealings with your works. Don't be suspicious, but don't be naive, either. Unintentional mistakes can easily happen, too. If your work is sold at inflated prices or to shady buyers, it can have disastrous consequences for you, as explained earlier. Always bear the consequences in mind.

And what is your longer-term perspective? Are your plans for the future compatible with the plans of your gallery? And how realistic are both your plans?

If you want to establish yourself as an international artist, it is advisable to enter into partnerships with other galleries abroad during the course of your career.

Successful artists sooner or later leave small galleries in favor of larger galleries. In most cases, this means the gallery couldn't or didn't want to grow as fast as the artist. And it is actually the fulfillment of the gallery's promise to its buyers, namely that its artist has become successful. Conversely, this means: If the artist didn't leave the gallery, the gallery's sales argument that he or she still had a great career ahead would have been a lie.

If your career requires you to leave your first gallery, this does not necessarily mean that the business contact will end. It may no longer be in first place, or it may change to a different form. But there's something nice about remembering who made your first steps possible.

At the end of the day, the collaboration between a gallery and an artist is purely a business relationship. On both sides! It should always be a win-win situation for both parties. If this no longer applies to you or if your perspectives have changed, then the relationship needs to end. And vice versa, if you don't generate sales, you have to accept that sooner or later you will be kicked out. And finally: As with any business, there are partners who are more honest and sincere but others who are less so. Only those who always maintain an overview remain in control of the situation.

There are many ways to bypass galleries today, and also some reasons why you might want to do so. For example, it's enormously tempting not to have to share the proceeds from your works. Nevertheless, if you want to become established and successful as an artist today and also sell your art, the route via a gallery is the more promising one.

9.4. Make your art collectible

There are artists whose works are not sellable because of their form or ephemerality, and there are artists who do not care whether their works can be sold or not. This may include biennale artists, as mentioned at the beginning of the book. First, let's make it clear that selling is virtually inevitable for a successful art career. But far more important is the realization that selling your art can have a very positive impact on your career. And here the focus is less on the money, but much more on the reputation and contacts you can gain through sales.

If selling doesn't interest you, then it is still important for you to realize that having "sellable" art is something positive. Therefore "sellable" should simply be replaced by the word "collectible" so as to avoid the term "sellable," which you may find unappealing.

The most extreme example is probably Tino Sehgal. His works are ephemeral "performances," he forbids any recording of them, and yet they can be collected. It is no secret that he is represented by a prestigious gallery and has sold his work to various museums. If he sells a work, there is no certificate when the agreement is concluded, nothing at all, at most a handshake with the artist. This shows that even he, the ultimate holdout, lets his works be collected. And with good reason: The institutions are among the most important influencers of the artistic canon, and so he cements his entry into the canon. You will probably have to offer a little more than a handshake, but this extreme example shows that "where there's a will, there's a way."

Making your art collectible is what allows you to maintain a lasting presence in the art world, become known, and be noticed by important people.

The impact of collections and collectors on your career

"The sales price achieved plays a much smaller role than the reputation of the collection."

When talking about collections, state collections at contemporary museums, but also private collections are meant here. Why should you care that works of yours end up in a collection?

First: You can benefit from their reputation. It makes other players in the art system understand that you must be taken seriously. The more significant the collection, the greater the impact. Now you just have to charmingly make sure that people know about it. It's the best advertising for you. Use it. You may also tell other potential buyers and partners directly and personally.

Second: The hope is that the collector or those responsible for the collection will tell their friends or patrons about the additional purchase, thus advertising you in a high-class environment. Sometimes, collections also have publicly available collection catalogs in which you are then listed. Furthermore, there is the possibility that your work will be shown in the context of collection exhibitions, meaning that the exhibition will be visited by many people and generate new "fans" for you.

Third: Especially for private collectors, the purchase of a work is a connecting element between the two of you. You can and should stay in contact with collectors and cultivate the relationship. Inform them regularly about your current work, but also occasionally ask them for advice or ask in a roundabout way if they can recommend you to a gallery or for participation in an exhibition at an art institution. They can help you realize complex artistic ventures or become a regular source of income for you. Remember: Collectors also benefit from the success of your career. If works of yours in the possession of a collector can be shown at exhibitions, this is good for their provenance and thus increases their value. So, it's only logical for the collector to give you a little help. If you are good friends, this is even more likely.

Collections, whether private or institutional, can be very influential. You can benefit from their reputation, and above all, personal contact with ambitious private collectors is very central to a successful career as an artist.

Making the non-collectible collectible

If you make huge installations, a collection probably won't waste limited and expensive storage space on an unknown artist. However, if you offer parts of the installation or side products for collecting, your chances of getting into a collection are much higher. Also consider that there are many smaller collections that can promote your name in art circles just as well but don't have such large capacities, neither in terms of storage space nor budget.

In practical terms, this means you must find a way to make your art "manageable" and collectible if it isn't by nature. There are countless ways to do this: You can look at and learn from other artists and you can find a lot of inspiration at international art fairs. One of the best examples already mentioned is Christo and Jeanne-Claude with their high quality sketches from their monumental projects.

In the case of installations, you may have parts of them that work on their own, or you may have side products that were created in the process or additionally produced and are related to the installation, whether through similar materials, techniques, or aesthetics. Other options include videos, models, and certificates.

In the case of performances, this can be documentation in the form of photos and videos, relics of the performance, and also certificates for a restaging/reenactment. You can make multiples/editions of anything. The sky's the limit. Whatever you do, it just has to be limited to a set number. There are endless possibilities and once you have figured it out, it's also easy to create new collectible works. It's a bit like merchandising.

9.5. Other ways to earn money as an artist

Besides selling your work, you have a variety of other ways to make money as an artist. However, only a few will transpire to be lasting or lucrative. You can combine some or even all of the below if you want to.

Funding and grants

There are a countless number of calls for applications for exhibitions with fees or expenses, grants, art prizes, residencies, subsidies, fellowships, and so on that will earn you money or save you money on living expenses, for example. Most have been created specifically to support artists and provide them with money or opportunities for exhibitions, studios, and travel. Either there are explicit calls for applications or you can apply for support with your own project.

Often, these opportunities are funded by the state or cultural foundations. Information about them can be found directly on the websites of the institutions. There are also various organizations and associations that try to collate the information and publish it in one place. If you are clever, you can raise funds from various sources, especially if you are aged between 20 and 30/35.

Percent for art and public art

The term "percent for art" refers to the idea of integrating art or attaching one or more works of art to buildings as part of large new construction or remodeling projects. Examples are artworks in schools but also art interventions in playgrounds, swimming pools, government buildings, housing developments, commercial buildings, and so on. In some countries, the state stipulates that approximately one percent of the construction costs of certain state-owned buildings must be spent on art, which is where the term "percent for art" comes from. In many places, both state and private property owners fund works of art on their buildings specifically and without being compelled to do so, because it is the thing to do.

Everyone knows public art. Almost everywhere in the world, it can be found in parks, squares and streets and should be accessible to people. Most of these pieces of art are large, permanent sculptures or installations.

These projects usually have large budgets and expenses are often reimbursed for the application process, too. As a result, this branch of art has established itself as an important source of income for many artists. Most often, these projects are put out to public bid.

Leverage your lifestyle

Being an artist can also be seen as a lifestyle that fascinates other people, and there are different ways to monetize it. Be it through a patron, a sugar daddy/mommy, crowdfunding, as an influencer, an ambassador/ advertiser for brands, and so on: It's up to you.

For the latter, there are currently a few examples of clever self-promotion on social media that are being monetized.

Accepting commissions

"Established artists have also developed ideas for well-known companies. They just don't shout it from the rooftops."

Artists are not infrequently asked about commissions in every conceivable field. Here, it is important that you know precisely where your work as an artist begins and where it ends. As an artist, you belong in the art context and once you leave it, you risk demeaning your work and damaging your reputation. Orders and commissions – even outside the art world – are acceptable, but it is important to handle them properly and with the required care. If necessary, you should simply use a pseudonym or insist on completing the project anonymously. Do not undermine your existence as an artist yourself.

9.6. Perfecting your résumé and your bibliography

"One relevant entry is worth more than ten virtually irrelevant ones."

On the one hand, we're talking here about the stages and events that form you and your artistic career. On the other hand, we're talking about the document that is often called a résumé and is part of your portfolio.

As mentioned several times, the résumé has established itself as one of the most important selection criteria for curators and jurors, but also for galleries and the like.

Résumé

Basically, the relevant stages and events in your résumé are as follows: art school, semester abroad, solo exhibitions, group exhibitions, grants, prizes/awards, residencies.

Since the résumé is so important today, it's clearly not advisable to leave these stages and events to chance. The point is not to collect as many stages and events as possible, but to be able to show a few relevant ones in your résumé. As is often the case, you should learn from other successful artists. What did they do at what time and what did it bring them? Every year, there are new grants, prizes, and so on. Old ones disappear or their relevance diminishes because the juries are no longer as high-caliber, or there may be other reasons.

Regularly respond to calls for applications. This will be an important part of your work as an artist and will take a lot of time. It's not uncommon for this paperwork to take up over half of your work time. Consider which calls for applications make sense for you at the current time and what would look good on your résumé. Government and institutional grants often have a higher reputation than private initiatives. Be aware that calls for applications that require an application fee are often dubious or irrelevant. However, there are a few notable exceptions.

It's hard to say how each stage and event will bring the greatest benefit to your career: By being in your résumé – in other words, contributing to your reputation? Or by the experience, the prize money, or similar? Or through the contacts you make in art school, during a residency, at an award ceremony, and so on? The fact is, all of them come down to what you make of them and whether you're willing to get the most out of them for your career.

If you're applying for prizes, grants, scholarships, etc., it's not just about winning them, it's also about the jury reading your name and getting to know your work. Jury members often repeat themselves or sit on multiple panels. If your work is constantly evolving, the jury will see that, whether you are nominated or not.

If we consider the résumé as a document, for example, as part of your portfolio or a call for applications, please be sure to include the following information, too: a listing of your percent for art projects, collaborations, and other projects that are not works in your portfolio but that you feel are important to mention. Also, your bibliography. Last but not least, you must mention the larger collections that contain works by you.

All this information and these stages and events, starting with your biography, must be grouped and listed chronologically in descending order, the most recent first, the oldest last. The more entries you have in your lists, the more you should remove from time to time, so that the relevant entries don't get lost among the unimportant ones. This document should always be up to date and, like your portfolio, available at all times, so you can send it immediately if needed.

Your bibliography

Your bibliography is a list of the catalogs and publications that deal with your work. Furthermore, selected texts and press articles can also be listed here.

Books, catalogs, and publications have lost an enormous amount of their influence in the digitally dominated world. However, this does not apply to the art world. Above all, books and catalogs are still as important here as they used to be.

The opportunity for books and catalogs to be published about your art work usually comes as your career progresses, but pay special attention to this as soon as you think the opportunity arises. This can be done, for example, as part of an institutional exhibition.

In the case of press articles, please note: It's not about general awareness, it's about awareness in the art world. Thus, it's important in which framework and publication organ the article was published. The best are always renowned professional journals or special sections of a few important daily newspapers and magazines. Otherwise, the article is, in fact, more or less irrelevant and really only belongs in your personal archive.

Basically, you should collect and keep everything that is published about your art and you. You should always back up and document digital articles and sources as they appear, in the form of a PDF file, screenshot, video, etc.

For example, if you have produced an artist's book or zine yourself, you may consider presenting it in more detail among the works in the portfolio, if appropriate, as it may be part of your artistic practice.

If there is a text or article that distinguishes you very favorably, because it comes from a prominent author or an important magazine (relevant in the art world), then you can include all of it in your portfolio.

Collections

If you have works in private as well as state collections, you can name the latter. If you do not yet have works in collections, it's no big deal and you simply omit this point in your document. However, it must be stressed that getting your works into collections is an enormously important topic, as explained in detail two chapters earlier.

Notes on calls for applications and open calls

"Applications are your bread & butter. You must invest a lot of time in them."

You will encounter calls for exhibitions, prizes/awards, grants, residencies, and so on many times, because they are an integral part of the art system today. They are often called "open calls." This means calls for applications for which (almost) any artist can apply. Sometimes you will need certain qualifications, occasionally you will need an advance invitation, but what they all have in common is that you ultimately have to apply for them yourself.

Miraculously, there have been more and more of these in recent years. On the one hand, this is, of course, to be welcomed, because it opens up many opportunities. On the other hand, however, it has created a lot of freeloaders and rotten apples who are really only interested in your money or misuse calls for their own interests. So, there is a certain amount of caution that needs to be exercised. In the past, it was actually easier and you could say that basically all calls where you didn't have to pay anything to register or participate were reputable, but this principle no longer applies everywhere.

You need to ask yourself the following questions right at the start: Who is the initiator of the call? Is there a registration fee? What costs can you expect if you win the bid? To what extent does the initiator benefit from his or her call?

Regarding registration fees: Many reputable applications are still free of charge. However, a few prestigious programs have introduced application fees, in order to process the increasing number of applications.

There have also been changes in participation costs. In the past, state arts funding programs often had their own residencies. However, the enormous increase in rents in many places has made them too expensive to maintain. In addition, some of these residencies were not used at all times, sometimes because the winning artists didn't take them up. As a result, many of these state residencies have been discontinued. Today, there are some recognized independent residencies for this purpose, which have good contacts with government and institutional arts funding programs. If you win such a residency as an artist, you theoretically have to pay the participation costs yourself, but you can claim the costs from the state or institutional funding programs. So, in the end you don't have to pay anything.

Regarding the reasons for open calls, it should be noted: Many remain committed to supporting artists, but some pursue other goals. Their initiators instrumentalize them for marketing purposes or see in them other economic or strategic advantages for their businesses. You should therefore always ask yourself: Does it make sense to be a part of this or not? Of course, it's not forbidden for initiators to benefit from open calls as well. Ideally, everyone should play with an open hand and a balanced win-win situation should be created for both parties.

Basically, this means you always have to inform yourself carefully and ask yourself how reputable the call is. Most of the time, you can find out who is behind the program and what their intentions are by looking at the website and doing a little research, which can convince you of their trustworthiness. A good indicator is also advertising. Reputable open calls rarely advertise, especially not on the Internet or Facebook, Instagram, or the like. Also, be careful if you can tell that a call for applications is trying to appeal to as many applicants as possible. At some point, it will be easy for the trained eye to separate the good from the bad.

9.7. Self-promotion

"The biggest fear is that we are insignificant. None of us wants to be insignificant."

Some very successful artists are self-promotion machines who specifically try to generate attention and also make no secret of the fact that they had PR agencies working for them for their breakthrough. Their strategy pays off, because they are successful with it.

Each artist must know for themselves how much they want to indulge in self-promotion. As always, the recommendation is: You should pull out all the stops! Otherwise, you will miss an important opportunity.

Basically, you have to ask yourself the question: How much self-promotion does it take for your contacts to keep you in mind? And the question that follows is: Are these contacts enough to advance your career? If not, can additional self-promotion give you the contacts you need? Or have you considered other avenues?

Go with the developments in society! Use the means of self-promotion of your time. Don't close your mind compulsively to self-promotion, unless you can really afford it and are already represented by Gagosian or Zwirner.

Your communication

"Work on your visibility."

Tell people what you're doing in your art career right now. Let them know that you are opening an exhibition, that you have won a prize, etc. It's important to use the media appropriately. In other words, don't overdo communication via particular channels. While you can post an Instagram story three times a day, you shouldn't write a short, informative e-mail more often than every two to eight weeks (ask yourself how many e-mails you really read). Posting banalities in social media stories may be acceptable, but you should never share them in e-mails.

Be aware of the transitory nature of information, but also of the flood of information, in the current age. Inform, but don't force information on anyone! If something is transient, it doesn't necessarily mean that it has less impact.

All of your self-promotion activities, through whatever channels, analog or digital, should have a certain stringency and continuity. The quality should meet the appropriate standards of the chosen medium. Your activities should give an insight into your work. How deep this insight is and where you draw the line to your private life is basically up to you, but there should always be a certain level of professionalism – although it might look more personal than professional. The image you give of yourself should correspond to your artist persona. As already explained in the chapter about the artist persona, it makes no sense to invent something that cannot be sustained over time. There is no general recipe. You can also look at what other artists do. However, there are very many bad or unprofessional examples, so you must be careful not to be misled by an inappropriate trend.

Please note: You definitely shouldn't hide your work, but don't give away every secret on your website or social media, either. On the one hand, because you want your fans to stay curious, and on the other hand, because you shouldn't give anyone an invitation to copy you. Artists have always been inspired by their peers. The sheer inexhaustibility and anonymity of the Internet have made it much easier to copy. Find a happy medium between self-promotion and secrecy.

Maintaining contacts

If you have found people who are interested in your art and you, that's great. But you also have to be able to win them over permanently. In addition to specifically arranged personal meetings, this can also be done using "PR and advertising." You have a wide range of options at your disposal: from a regular e-mail newsletter, to social media, sending invitation cards to your exhibitions by regular mail, and even events at your studio.

A personal contact list is indispensable for maintaining contacts. The best way to do this is to use an Excel list. Assign a group to each contact; this defines how closely you are connected, for example: friends, business, and VIP. This way you can quickly send invitations for the exclusive pre-opening of your solo show or your less formal birthday party. For each contact, write how and where you met, including a few important keywords about the person, so the list remains useful even after a few years.

While this chapter on maintaining contacts may end here, it does not do so in the real world, but continues there in the form of networking.

Social media

For some time now, there have been many young, ambitious artists who have been using social media in particular to attract attention. With sometimes ingenious strategies, such as those used by Amalia Ulman, they have smoothly expanded the concept of art and entered the artistic canon. But there are countless other examples of how mainly young artists have been able to establish themselves with the help of digital media.

The "Art Basel and UBS Global Art Market Report" in early 2020 highlights how important social media, especially Instagram, has become even in buying decisions, and it's no secret that many curators, galleries, and collectors intensively search for new talents on Instagram. But it's not just Instagram: Outside of North America and Western Europe, other channels dominate in part, which are (still) not very common here. In addition, the digital world, for example in East Asia, is even more firmly anchored in society and has a greater influence.

If social media is used for self-promotion, rather than as an art form, it's about showing those around you that you're a hardworking artist and providing insight into your creative processes and artistic persona. This can be done with varying degrees of effort. Some of what comes across as cheeky and effortless on social media channels is actually staged with a lot of effort. But with a little practice and a reduced dose of ego and perfectionism, the amount of time you devote to social media channels can be reduced tremendously. Much of the activity of numerous artists on social media is definitely a waste of time and goes beyond self-promotion, and the actual benefit to their careers is rather small. As a social phenomenon and pastime, it's okay, but as an artist, you should make better use of your time.

Basically, it's not about how many followers you have or how much attention you generate. What is more important is the quality of your followers or audience and their relevance in the art world and art system.

Studio events

Studio events seem to have gone a bit out of fashion in certain circles – rather unfairly, because they are a simple, fun, and effective way of maintaining contacts and self-promotion. They can also be easily combined with a gallery collaboration. At the studio event, your gallery should be present and be the point of contact for all sales.

Website, business cards and the 20-second pitch

As noted in the "commandments," it is important that people can find you when they look you up on Google. And people must be able to get in touch with you. This can be achieved in a number of ways. The simplest, most effective, and professional way is to have your own website with your name as the URL. Quite often, this is also the only way to ensure that your search result does not disappear among all the others with the same or similar names. If in doubt, a website with only one page, your name, and e-mail address will suffice. Of course, it must be clear that it is about you, the artist.

Business cards may be old fashioned, and yet they work better than you think in certain circles. They cost almost nothing and are also sometimes handy for additional notes to the recipient. Your art may be creative, but hold back on creativity with your business card.

If someone spontaneously asks for your work, you are welcome to show it on your cell phone, under the following conditions: Your phone's technology is up to date, your photos make an impression, and your work can be experienced in some way, albeit in a reduced form. Finding photos should not take more than 10 seconds and do not show videos longer than 15 seconds. The easiest way is to have a folder with photos/videos or a PDF portfolio ready for this – or your website is designed for mobile devices and you have fast mobile Internet.

9.8. Bureaucracy

Being creative in the studio is great, but even artists can't avoid desk work, if they want to be successful. Here are a few, but helpful, keywords. But always keep yourself updated, as things change every now and then and vary from country to country.

Professional associations

Professional associations can help you in many matters as an artist, especially with bureaucratic issues.

Accounting and taxes

You can't start early enough with your own accounting. Usually, by the time you begin, it's already too late. Four things are important. First: Record all your earnings in one central place. Second: Collect all your receipts, documents, and bills for all expenses such as materials, external production costs, tools, literature, transportation, insurance, rent for work space, telephone, museum visits, travel, restaurants, etc. in a central location in a file folder or box. Third: If you earn more than $10,000 per year, get yourself an accountant immediately. Fourth: If you earn more than $100,000 per year, go to an accountant who is very familiar with the problems (also the personal ones) of artists. If you follow these four principles, you'll be on the safe side. If not, you're guaranteed to run into huge problems sooner or later.

Sales tax

As mentioned above, sales tax must usually be paid to the state when artworks are sold. Most of the time, the gallery takes care of that. However, if you sell from your studio, it becomes your obligation, although in most countries you are exempt if your turnover is below a certain amount. (Your turnover is all your income in a calendar year, without deductions.)

In some countries, special sales tax rates apply to art, or art may even be taxed differently depending on whether it is sold directly from the studio or through a gallery.

If your works are sold from Europe to the United States, for example, no sales tax is payable in Europe. However, the buyer must independently pay the import tax to the United States.

Copyright and resale rights

In English-speaking countries, the term "copyright" is mostly used for a bundle of rights. Whereas in many other regions, a distinction is made between "copyright," i.e. "right of use," which is mainly concerned with monetization and, for example, "author's rights" or "moral rights," which protect the personal and reputational rights of the artist. This was first regulated in the Berne Convention for the Protection of Literary and Artistic Works of 1886 and is actually valid worldwide. These rights automatically belong to the artist upon completion of the work of art (except for commissioned works in some countries), and are usually valid for many decades beyond the artist's death.

If an artwork is sold, the copyright nevertheless remains with the artist, unless he or she expressly sells this along with the work. The buyer of an artwork is therefore not normally entitled to sell, for example, postcards with the artwork without the artist's permission. This is why you often see the phrase "courtesy of the artist" next to images of artworks. In order to be able to sue for a copyright infringement in court, for example in the United States, the copyright must first be registered there, although the artist is clearly entitled to it.

Normally, it's counterproductive to your career to keep anyone from publishing pictures of your artwork. After all, it's the best advertising for you.

In some countries remuneration that you are due through copyright, for example when photos of your works get published, can be claimed through copyright collecting societies on your behalf.

In certain countries, resale rights exist, which means that if your work is sold on the secondary market in such a country, you get a share of the resale proceeds if you assert your copyright there.

10. Dealing with success and failure

"Success attracts success."

In the beginning, you are the unknown little artist who depends on the goodwill of other players in the art system. Success and failure are very close to each other and can alternate in short intervals. But ultimately, it's the long-term trend that will determine whether you will succeed. So, don't let setbacks demotivate you, but take them seriously. From both your failures and your successes, you can draw conclusions about your art, your artistic persona, yourself as a person, and about the art system itself. Learn from them and use this knowledge to your advantage. Nothing just happens. There is an explanation for everything.

"Use the drive that success gives you to reach new heights, or stop the negative vibes of failure before they consume you."

Think of your artistic career as a vehicle that you have to push with a lot of effort. Once it's moving, you'll have to pedal hard to maintain or increase the speed. If you stop pedaling, the speed will decrease and the vehicle will soon come to a standstill. It's the same with a successful career as an artist.

Success has its responsibilities. Once you are successful, more attention will be paid to you and your work. Your work will probably be judged more critically, just by being seen by more people. Showing and/or selling more art usually means having to produce more art. As a rule, expectations of you will rise. New, additional tasks will be imposed on you. Working with conviction, as you used to, will quickly be replaced by the pressure to succeed, which can wear you down. What if you can't serve the market? What if you run out of ideas, or the quality of your work becomes poor?

Success not only attracts (false) friends, it also brings you envious people and resentment, which can sometimes be exhausting to the point of damaging your reputation. As already explained in the chapter about strategies, the "wolf in sheep's clothing" approach helps, at least at the beginning. You can also make clear to your friends that sooner or later they can also benefit from your success. In other words, you can adopt the "form a group" strategy.

Nevertheless, it is helpful to understand that success changes your focus. Depending on what point you are at in your career, you will have different interests and priorities. For example, if you're working toward an important exhibition, you may not have time for that beer with your artist friends, even though you still value them and would actually enjoy spending time with them. And it can affect other people and decisions, too. You should be aware of these behavior patterns and address them specifically to avoid misunderstandings.

"Only when you are invited to relevant exhibitions on your own merits as an artist have you definitely achieved success."

Failure is part of your work as an artist: As mentioned before in the section on perfecting your résumé, for example, being rejected in calls for applications is not inherently bad, because the jury members and curators get to know you through your application.

Think about why you have experienced failures. Analyze specific situations and ask yourself: What was lacking? Is my body of work of substandard quality? Is my subject matter not interesting? Am I too old or too young? Do I lack experience? Do I not have the right connections? Or does the jury just not like the look of me?

Quite often, the reason for your rejection is not so much your work, but many other criteria mentioned in this book. It takes a lot of perseverance. One acceptance can be followed by ten rejections – that's absolutely normal.

Unfortunately, when applying for art schools, prizes/awards, scholarships, and so on, you're not told why you were rejected. Given the huge number of applications, this is completely understandable, but not very helpful nor sustainable. Nevertheless, you can always somehow find out where you stand. For example, when applying to an art school, you can discuss your rejected portfolio with the students there. In the case of a prize or scholarship, you can analyze the nominees' work and résumés and compare them to yours. And there are many more ways to contextualize yourself.

If necessary, reread this book so that you understand the interrelationships in the art system and can apply them to your career as an artist.

"Doubt is normal. Try to find a happy medium between ignorance and reflection, and try to harness the process of doubting in a controlled way."

If you're going through a hard time or you get stuck in a train of thought or entrenched a problem, it can often be hard to get out of it. The fact is, there is virtually always a way out. The first question is whether you are capable of analyzing the problem objectively, the second is whether you are ready to bear the consequences, and the third is whether you can muster the necessary strength to do so. You are responsible for your own happiness.

Crises

Every artist has a crisis at some point. Some even have several. Often, crises are caused by self-doubt and being ignored, for instance, if you haven't had an exhibition in a while and no one is interested in your art. Or you may be experiencing a production standstill and don't know what to produce next. Of course, there are many more triggers. The fact is: Crises are absolutely normal. The important thing is that you learn how to deal with them. Train yourself to avoid them – but if you're ever in the middle of a crisis, accept it and come out stronger the other side. Develop your personal crisis management strategy. A common practice is to turn crises into periods of recovery and inspiration. Or take a step back and change direction. Crises are an important part of self-reflection. Talking about them a lot also helps. Talk to friends about your art. Don't bother them endlessly with your negative vibes, because you'll lose important conversational partners, but do talk to them about your work. Speak with fellow artists about their work – that can also help you "find yourself" again.

The biggest advantage of being an artist over other professions is that you're officially allowed to have crises. Nevertheless, it is advisable to maintain a certain professionalism and discretion.

11. Plan B or exit?

"A friend of mine once said: 'The only reason I'm still creating art is because there's no going back to normal life!'"

Becoming a successful artist is a huge challenge. But probably an even bigger challenge is to accept that you won't manage to be a successful artist and to give up striving to become one without becoming bitter and rejecting the art world.

As this book hopefully pointed out to you, there are many factors that determine a successful career as an artist, so don't take it too personally if it doesn't work out.

But it's not just about admitting that your dream failed. The art system has probably become your home. Here, you have your contacts, your friends, your interests, and so on. Once you're in, it's not so easy to get out. But there is also no point in delaying the exit from life as a professional artist for many years.

If, after 10 years, you still haven't made it onto the escalator of success, then it's unlikely to get any better in the future. At some point, enough is definitely enough. Of course, there are always exceptions, but why should you of all people be lucky?

"Accept who and what you are."

Furthermore, not everyone can or wants to live or survive as an independent artist in the long run.

The question also arises, in which league did you want to make the breakthrough? Perhaps a career as a national or regional artist will do after all. Each league has its advantages and disadvantages, or obligations and freedoms.

Maybe you can take a longer break, earn money somewhere else for the time being, and later get completely reorganized with a clear-cut strategy. But remember, it doesn't get easier with age.

Rejecting the path of the successful and professional artist doesn't mean you have to give up your art. You can continue as an amateur artist or use your skills in other jobs. Some "failed" artists have become renowned gallery owners, art critics, or curators.

"I think kids are the easiest exit strategy!"

Jobs for artists

Here are some (related) professions for artists that are obvious and valuable and that you can consider if you want to quit as an independent artist or are looking for an art-related side income. For some, of course, you'll need to get further qualifications or work experience. The list does not claim to be complete.

Art in education
Teaching art practically or theoretically can be a fine and valuable occupation that can provide you with a regular and secure income. You could be an art teacher at a regular school, a professor at an art school, or you could teach privately organized courses.

Assistants, lecturers on contracts, professors of art theory, workshop managers, etc. from art academies/schools should also be mentioned here.

Art in the cultural sector
Here, of course, there are the most opportunities and you already know many players in the art sector from this book. Maybe you can imagine becoming a gallery owner, curator, or critic.
Some options have not been mentioned yet, although they are important for all processes in the art system: for example, art handlers, who physically handle artworks. Their job involves setting up and dismantling exhibitions and working in logistics, transport, and warehouse management. Or you may consider becoming a curatorial assistant, an assistant to artists for a gallery (artist liaison), an office assistant, or the like.

There are opportunities to work in art mediation and education in museums or collections. Or your career path may take you to a position in a governmental department for art and culture.

Then there is the artist's assistant. Successful artists usually have a large studio or workshop, and so they need staff to assist them – but artist's assistants are needed in art production companies, too.

Last but not least, stage designers, scenic artists, and set designers in theater and film, as well as signwriters should be mentioned.

Art in the healthcare sector
Art as a form of therapy has proven to be very helpful in assisting people in a wide variety of life situations. Applications are wide-ranging, from occupational therapy in senior care to the work of trauma recovery specialists.

Art in the private sector, outside the art sector
You may also want to consider slightly less art-specific jobs requiring additional skills, such as being an assistant or art director in the advertising, film, gaming, or fashion industry. Other opportunities include interior design, industrial and furniture design, or working as a photographer's assistant.

12. The death of the artist

Let us make one thing clear right away: The chances of you being discovered after your death are practically zero, because there are more than enough artists around today. If you're not well known during your lifetime and/or you don't have a huge stockpile of high-quality works, you'll just quietly disappear. But a huge stockpile alone is not enough – your works must have a place in the artistic canon and be specifically passed on to an enterprising foundation or an estate executor.

Here are some notes for successful artists – although all artists should take the following lines to heart and absorb them into their consciousness.

Unlike most other professions and careers, artists, if they want to and are still mentally and physically fit, can and very often do work until old age or death. Being an artist is usually a lifelong vocation.

This is, of course, very nice in principle, but it can mean that artists do not plan their departure from the world of work and so miss the last chance to actively intervene in their career. Furthermore, they may avoid dealing with important matters that can become a problem for their descendants.

"Your career doesn't stop when you die."

You can get together with experts to draw up a concept of how your death and estate will be handled – steps that can have a significant impact on your posthumous career. The news of your death alone should prompt the media to cover you. Your estate can benefit from this momentum.

Be sure to have an up-to-date inventory that goes to the estate executor. Generally, the more clutter you leave behind, the more expensive the cleanup will be. It can destroy important funds, and thus affect the estate's ability to operate. However, you should not discard works unnecessarily. The estate will be pleased to have anything it can convert into money sooner or later.

Settle your estate early. It's not just about your career as an artist, but also about the fact that, depending on where you live, inheritance taxes may be due on all of your works that were in your possession up to your death. Depending on what your market prices are at the time, a huge amount might suddenly become payable. Failure to consider this can lead to major problems.

The basic questions are: Who will inherit your remaining works? Who will receive the copyright for your work? Who should administer your estate? And so on. There are several ways to settle your estate. Take care of it early, get advice from artist friends and experts.

Closing words

"Keep enjoying your work – joy is more important than success."

This book gives you the knowledge you need to succeed in the jungle of the art world. Even if it doesn't seem to address all of your personal situation, it should have sharpened and trained your mind to gain and fill in the missing knowledge yourself.

The fact is that, statistically, only a single-digit percentage of art school graduates go on to earn a full living as artists. Hopefully, this book will help to ensure that perhaps a few percent more will do so in the future – and if not, it will at least save some artists from pointless and haphazard wandering in the jungle of the art world.

A summary for the forgetful:
Work extremely hard. Never put your ego before your art or your career. Always reflect on your work. It must be absolutely top-quality and contemporary. Expand and maintain your friendships in the art world. Let the art world know what you're working on regularly. Make your résumé exciting (study abroad, residencies, etc.). Look for good opportunities (prizes/awards, residencies, exhibitions, etc.) to prove yourself. Go to where the action is in the art world. Don't stop working extremely hard and with focus. Wait until the right offers (exhibitions, galleries, etc.) come along. Go for it. Work even more.

As you have read, it is possible to approach an artist's career with determination and to plan it precisely. Whether you have the financial means to do so, whether you can demonstrate sufficient energy and stamina, and whether you are capable of making certain decisions not in your personal interest but in that of your artistic career, is up to you. Everything for art!